PHENOMENOLOGY OF DECOLONIZING THE UNIVERSITY:

Essays in the Contemporary Thoughts of Afrikology

Zvikomborero Kapuya

Edited by Tendai R. Mwanaka

Mwanaka Media and Publishing Pvt Ltd,
Chitungwiza Zimbabwe
*
Creativity, Wisdom and Beauty

Publisher: Mmap
Mwanaka Media and Publishing Pvt Ltd
24 Svosve Road, Zengeza 1
Chitungwiza Zimbabwe
mwanaka@yahoo.com
www.africanbookscollective.com/publishers/mwanaka-media-and-publishing
https://facebook.com/MwanakaMediaAndPublishing/

Distributed in and outside N. America by African Books Collective
orders@africanbookscollective.com
www.africanbookscollective.com

ISBN: 978-1-77929-608-5
EAN: 9781779296085

© Zvikomborero Kapuya 2019

All rights reserved.
No part of this book may be reproduced or transmitted in any form or by any means, mechanical or electronic, including photocopying and recording, or be stored in any information storage or retrieval system, without written permission from the publisher

DISCLAIMER
All views expressed in this publication are those of the author and do not necessarily reflect the views of *Mmap*.

Mwanaka Media and Publishing Editorial Board:

Publisher/ Editor-in-Chief: Tendai Rinos Mwanaka
mwanaka13@gmail.com
East Africa and Swahili Literature: Dr Wanjohi wa Makokha
makokha.justus@ku.ac.ke
East Africa English Literature: Andrew Nyongesa (PhD student)
nyongesa55.andrew@gmail.com
East Africa and Children Literature: Richard Mbuthia
ritchmbuthia@gmail.com
Legal Studies and Zimbabwean Literature: Jabulani Mzinyathi
jabumzi@gmail.com
Economics, Development, Environment and Zimbabwean Literature: Dr Ushehwedu Kufakurinani ushehwedu@gmail.com
History, Politics, International relations and South African Literature: Antonio Garcia antoniogarcia81@yahoo.com
North African and Arabic Literature: Fethi Sassi sassifathi62@yahoo.fr
Gender and South African Literature: Abigail George
abigailgeorge79@gmail.com
Francophone and South West African Literature: Nsah Mala
nsahmala@gmail.com
West Africa Literature: Macpherson Okpara
chiefmacphersoncritic@gmail.com
Media studies and South African Literature: Mikateko Mbambo
me.mbambo@gmail.com
Portuguese and West Africa Literature: Daniel da Purificação
danieljose26@yahoo.com.br

DEDICATION

This book is dedicated to Sharon Rutendo Ruswa, Simbarashe Murape Chitsinde, the late Cheikh Anta Diop, Steve Bantu Biko and Frantz Fanon.

CONTENTS

Preface..8
Chapter 1: Phenomenology of Decolonizing the University; An Introduction..10
Chapter 2: Objectivity/Subjectivity/Coloniality of University-Ontology of the "Other"..................................22
Chapter 3: Historical Materialism of the Decolonial-Turn-Liberating African Intellectualism..................................39
Chapter 4; Reflection of Decolonial Scholarship; Critical Thinking Perspective..60
Chapter 5: Social Transformation; An Empirical Survey of Midlands State University on Decolonizing the University.....................75
Chapter 6: Redefine the Image of 'African Being' from the 'Other'-Thinking Decolonizing the University..................................96
Bibliography...109
Publisher's list...117

ACKNOWLEDGMENTS

My special acknowledges goes to the Almighty God. I would like to appreciate my late parents, Patrick Kapuya and Caroline Chitsinde for their unwavering support from wherever the world there are right now. My gratitude to Midlands State University, for imparting me with social and scientific knowledge about political philosophy in four years of study and help me in the development of the theory of African being and Decolonizing the University. I would like to Acknowledge, Richard Mahomva, Mrs J.T Mudzamiri, Dr T Mude, Professor P Chigora, Dr A Chilunjika, Mr S Moyo and Professor Charles Tembo for their unwavering support in the development of Afrocentric theory in education and rethinking African political philosophy.. To the Vengesayi Architect for their financial support in my academic adventure, I am forever grateful. I would like to acknowledge my family, for their love and support of my passion in literature and friends for their support and encouragements in the journey of producing this theory. Not to forget Sharon Rutendo Ruswa for her support, motivation and being a pillar of strength during the course of research of this book. To my undergraduates and postgraduates classmates, their industrious support is greatly appreciated.

I Can No Longer Breathe

I stand out in the midst of your power and supremacy degraded by your battering and hatred for me because I am...
False lies perpetuated in classrooms and lecture rooms, to make me feel insignificant and worthless.
Told that my story begins and ends with your supreme nature, told that being dark skinned is a tyranny, an umbilical cord waiting to be cut and destroyed- are the physical ropes and chains you tied my ancestors with.
Still strapped and chained like a slave, like a dog chained to Magogo's gate. Mentally enslaved is what it is called...
Once again, my mother and my father reduced to nothing but labour.
Stripped of my dignity, my integrity gone and nowhere to be seen HENCE I CAN NO LONGER BREATHE (Masisi 2016)

Preface

The idea of decolonization remains a complex theory, with so much confusion and misunderstandings, various scholars claim to be fanatics of this theory however are still using the same Eurocentric methodology in analysis. Of course it is quite impressive to have numerous stand points and debates, as to tests, experiment this theory in social laboratory. The constructive criticism helps to refine understanding of the epistemic freedom theory, however it is a pity to see academias even criticizing this theory, planning academic conspiracy and assassinations, to African scholars who are still hanging on colonial apology stand point, they don't realize their fierce critic to decolonial thought is not 'homicide' but 'suicide' which means there are killing themselves and thus performs menticide. The dawn of new horizon in African public space, is critically informed by the shift of images, dreams and visions towards African Renaissance. The continent is performing badly, there's ceaseless wars, serious abject poverty and political instability, these catastrophes are owed to the idea of 'coloniality' hence to move forward, and unleash us from the chains of epistemic slavery there's need to decolonize academic spaces. The diagnosis of this problem, provides a hilarious moments to the African political physician, who now have a solution. The previous generation spend years of researches, but the current definition of African scholars finds the cure of African problems. The cure is movement towards epistemic freedom. This book is written in decolonial humanities and social science format, but it doesn't necessarily mean it belongs to those disciplines, it is a political-revolutionary book worth to be read by every person who has the interest in dismantling Eurocentric canon of thoughts. It contains intellectual jargons, from human science disciplines, the thrust is to locate itself to the intellectual society since these are most victimized groups, detached from their roots. The discipline is now long overdue as academic discourse, but it's now time to claim political landscape to grow the idea in every individual in Africa, and the global south. The idea might take long, since we need to dismantle the existing world view which is nearly seven centuries old, hence to re-establish and develop the epistemic project- it might be a piecemeal movement or even radical but towards the goal of freeing our minds. Decolonizing the university, means more than to narrowly focus on Africanizing the university, it also aims to free Europeans from the mental delusion of African images constructed by their forefathers. The issue of polycentric template of epistemologies cultivates the humanistic legacies within the perspectives of decoloniality.

Zvikomborero Kapuya

Chapter One: Phenomenology of decolonizing the University; An Introduction

Phenomenology- (De-Colonialty)

"Postanthropocentricism, posthumanism and Post-Cartesianism are more about cannibalistic deconstructing and decentering of African human beings/bodies than they are about decolonizational/decoloniality as understood in Africa's historical context..., decolonization should be about recentering those that were colonially decentered and deconstructed" (Nhemachena; 2018).

The application of phenomenology approach to the study of contemporary Africa proved useful in understanding the rationality and logic of decolonizing epistemologies. Phenomenology questions the existence and establishes an epistemic relationship between the subject and as a dominant issue in post-colonial global south, various scholars provide proposals and frameworks on how to decolonize knowledge, from radical and moderate point of view. The groups are divided into three groups; The first group is of Afrocentric scholars based on redefining black identities and historical consciousness of Africans in Africa and Africans in Diaspora, The second group emerge from Caribbean scholars' proposal of the aspect of 'decoloniality' and 'boarder thinking" and the last group is of Pan African scholars in Africa advocating for decolonizing languages, literature, history and territorial boarders. This aspect of decolonizing the knowledge production is not a closed issue, aiming to Africanize the university but to develop a polycentric paradigm in the discourse of epistemic global economy. Professor Artwell Nhemachema, a distinguished anthropologist put forward a theoretical framework of understanding the post-primitive (Post-anthropocentricism), post humanism and post-Cartesian, that simply explains post-modern world in comprehending the dominant issues of decolonization. The concept 'de-colonization' is the main theme of post-colonial Africa whereby the path to attain the absolute freedom of the 'mind', 'soul' and 'body' is designed in various social movements and institutions.

Interpreting the normative theory of Arab-conquest, slave trade, colonialism and neo-colonialism to provide a hermeneutic dimension of intellectual vacuum of the black nation. Dibash (2015) ask, "Can Non-Europeans Think?, Mignolo respond in the foreword of the book, "Yes we can", referring to the matrix of coloniality and decoloniality of knowledge(s). The transcendental thoughts, phenomenology provides a basic epistemology through reducing the distance between the subject and the object, and comprise it in the concept of phenomenon (mental and physical). Hence the learning structures at universities influence the object and the subject, that influence the development of the decoloniality of the university theory. The politics of knowing in the world has been dominated by the western world, and influences their way of thinking and aesthetics to the rest of the world. Social sciences and humanities knowledge structure, premised on the foundation of European cannon of knowledge, whereby theorist who shape thoughts in those disciplines, are from five countries, namely Germany, Great Britain, United States of America, Italy and France and also ancient Greek philosophers. This issue, midwives the theory of social change based on decolonizing the university and re-centering social subalterns in global economy of knowledge(s). The dominant issue of decolonizing the university parade in global academic society and social ecology, help in developing contemporary thoughts in Africology interdisciplinary views. It started on the justification of existence of African civilization, African philosophy, African Literature and various myths that were dominant for centuries about Africa. This book is focusing on the phenomenology, the scientific and social nature of the concept of decolonizing the university in African society and expands the epistemological scope of the study. The book seeks to achieve two broad issues, (1) to understand the Eurocentric epistemic construction in colonial and post-colonial times and (2) to develop decolonial alternatives from the already existing literature and align it with practical realities. This can be achieved through thorough literature review of new-emerging themes of African historiography, literature, Afrocentric, decoloniality theory and explaining the trajectories of 'coloniality and decoloniality'. Luso-Hispanic scholars have already started to work on this subject, which produce a theoretical foundation and literature reference of this paradigm. Walter D Mignolo, Nelson Maldonado-Torres, Ramon Grosfoguel, Arturo Escobar, Annibal Quinjano and Sylvia Wynter, just to mention a few, play an important role in providing the volume of literature on the concept of decolonizing the university through introducing academic concepts such as decoloniality, modernity, coloniality and epistemicide. Other historic scholars write within the dominant oppression of global epistemology are key important figures in the art and science of knowing. Cheikh Anta Diop, Kwasi Wiredu and other notable African scholars contribute immensely to the development of this theory. The phenomenology of decolonizing the university as an interdisciplinary thought about the university education, focusing on theories of social transformation and the need to answer various questions about epistemology of the study. Little publication has been put in place in the academic and social affairs about this issue, this book focuses on unpacking the reality of the study in adding literature and also try to venture in marginalized "other", the society, to create meaning not only to academic world for referencing and writing but plays a critical role in practical social change.

Pan African Hangover

Pan Africanism played a decisive role in decolonizing political space. Nationalist leaders develops strategies on establishing political and economic independence however they failed to diagnose the real problem of the complex of global coloniality, coloniality of being and the 'epistemcide'. This issue informs the thrust of this book, whereby Pan African movement failed to continue in national building, wrestled down the undiscovered coloniality of epistemologies.

> "The reason for the sad mental state is that we have been fighting against the evil of colonization as an economic and political problem rather than a total conceptual distortion, leading to confusion" (Asante, 2007; p10).

Molefe Kete Asante normative observation occupy the statement problem of this study. Since the beginning of decolonization and nationalism in former colonized states, leaders and former colonial subjects treat colonialism superficially, only as political and economic issue. However, this study unpacks the realities of colonialism as a living anatomy in African being in the period of emptiness observed by Hannah Arendt social philosophy (No longer political colonialism, not yet Independence). Political colonialism exists invisibly, however mental slavery perpetuate the period of emptiness since the quest for independence remains unfinished in critic of what nationalists believes. The university operates in Eurocentric knowledge(s) that problematize the fabrication of new thoughts in Africa. Issues such as racism, white supremacism and modernity remains unquestioned in the so-called universities of the South. In this regard alienation and mental confusion rein the system and affect the discourse of Africanity in African universities. Yes there's 'Africanization' of the university, renaming and dismantling of racism but the issue of Eurocentric paradigm hegemony dominates the academic world. The University approaches the world as society of scholars came together in search for truth about the nature of the society, science and humanities. University of Al Qarawiyyin in 859AD existed as intellectual society awarding degrees to the students who successfully completed their study and research on truth of the meaning of the world. In antiquity those institutions were there but served different purposes like religious training, since theological beliefs influenced the thinking of the societies. In Egypt, Mali, Greece and various societies they formulated learning communities mentoring talents such as art and vocational skills to produce critical mass and state existence that create comprehensions in the beginning of Egyptian philosophy. Egyptian philosophy influenced global learning societies in Greece, Israel and other parts of the world. George G.M James penned a book *"Stolen Legacy; Egyptian Origins of Greek Philosophy"* in 1954 as an intellect volume in an attempt to restore the African glory of the past that was distorted by Eurocentric writers. The book largely focuses on how European writers deny the pedigree of Greek philosophy as originated in Egypt. Egypt was the center of civilization and scholastic invention in antiquity, in the disciplines of law, medicine, mathematics, architecture, theology and philosophy.

The author presents the argument of the demise of Kemetic empire through series of invention from the Arabs, Persians, Greeks and later on Romans that demystifies the historic contribution of Egypt in scholastic World (William; 1992). Learning system was structured on the question of what is God. Does he really Exist? What is universe? Is there any other races? This was the dominant questions in intellectual societies, some of the publications found in Timbuktu believed to be first organized learning institutions, serves the purpose in developing Islamic philosophy and study of Quran, the religious wisdom of Islam. Issues of studying Astrology as the main priority, creates an advent of the word universe-hence university, since the community of scholars, truth seekers focus on the question of universe. The 'concept of university' revolve in myth, since social science disciplines are dominated by only five western countries theorists. Germany, Britain, France, Italy and United States of America theorists dominate disciplines such as Philosophy, Political Science, Sociology and Anthropology and apply the Cartesian epistemic thoughts. For instance in Political Science discipline, premised on the Eurocentric cannon of thoughts, Niccollo Machiavelli (Italy), Thomas Hobbes (Great Britain), Jean Jacques

Rousseau (France), John Locke (Great Britan), James Madison (USA) and Greek Philosophers such as Aristotle, Plato and Socrates, dominate schools of thought. The named scholars, invent theories such as Democracy, Socialism, State of Nature, Absolutism and Constitutionalism; and these theories dominate the courses and modules of political science, hence this aspect led to the universalization of Eurocentric knowledge(s) and provincializes the rest. Against this background the objectivity and subjectivity of university education designed to dominate the minds of other parts of the world. University defined as a community of researchers, scholars and tutors dedicating their life in search for truth in natural and human science and, has a social significance through promoting social and economic progress. Earning University degree has social impact in societies, since it raise the status of earners of university qualification from bachelors to doctoral studies.

The main question is, what is the meaning of university in African perspective?. This creates a problematic concept, since university as the citadel of knowledge in Africa plays a pivotal role in alienating scholars in Africa, and creates the other and non-thinking beings, conditioned to think in Eurocentric world view. Instead of producing critical thinkers, new elites and bourgeoisie in Africa emerge and focuses only on their status rather than promote the growth of ideas for the betterment of the society. The main cause of this is the dominant Eurocentric epistemologies across all faculties and disciplines in African Universities. The subverse conundrum in the discourse of university problematize knowledge making in universities and traumatize genuine knowledge making in universities of the south. This book focuses on conceptual and empirical research on coloniality and decoloniality of the university education in Africa, and what are the ramifications to be put forward in order to consume the gulf between educational theories and society. This theory, many publications just focuses on social critic and academics without social relevance, is the main thrust of this book to engage in social relevance of the phenomenology of decolonizing the university.

The Structure and Contending Issues of the work

This book is divided into five chapters, as to achieve the aims of understanding coloniality and decoloniality as well as developing the social theory of decolonizing the university and create 'thinking beings' in Africa. Chapter 2 is entitled, *"Subjectivity/Coloniality of the University-The Ontology of the other"*. The so called coloniality perpetuates itself as living anatomy in Africa's academic society. This chapter focuses on elucidating the coloniality of the university, constructing diverse thoughts from already published materials and develops the logic. The phenomenology of the coloniality of the university presages mental slavery and thus it promotes alienation to the educated elite. This chapter explains how Europe derail African knowledge systems in academic communities. Through social and political conquest, expanding the geopolitics of knowing used as the methodology in consolidating colonialism. The mindset and the art of thinking affected by the Europeans as to buttress their geopolitical expansion. This issue problematizes the contemporary learning system, whereby the intellectual community is alienated from African being to create the 'Other'. Africa is no longer self but other-self. The ontological creation of inferiority, death of African personality (menticide) and the phenomenology of the other-being explained as coloniality of being affect social transformation and the meaning of independence in African discourse. This agony creates new elites of educated bourgeoisie that distances themselves from their roots.

The main purpose of this chapter is to juxtapose the marginalization of the 'Other' from the 'Other' in creating the theory with social and practical meaning. The concept of universe in knowledge making institutions lacks the construction of the subverse in the body of knowledge(s), since western thoughts are celebrated as important epistemic paradigm in global knowledge making. In consolidating colonization and global hegemony, geopolitics of knowing extended from western world as the center of every civilization to other parts of the world. This global structure create classes in the world, those "Who fabricate knowledge" and "those who abide to it"-that destroys the social determinants of humanity, divide the society and enhance subjectivity and objectivity. The ontology of the other-reconstructed in African phenomenon which procreates the mindset of Anti-Africanism in academic society. Coloniality of knowledge, linguistic imperialism, coloniality of being and power, are major concepts to be analyzed in this chapter. Reconstructing thoughts and arguments to build the comprehension of Coloniality of university and how it is hampering germination of new thoughts.

Chapter 3, focuses on conceptual framework of exhuming the evolutions of decoloniality from the hermeneutical and phenomenological paradigm. *"Historical Materialism of De-colonial Turn-Liberating African (Black) Intellectualism"*. The intellectual potency of global south as it is explained in chapter 2. This chapter's main objective is to trace the historical evolution of the concept and social movement of decolonization as historical events. Integrating global South spiritual movement of decolonization, creating avenues for the need and realization of decolonizing the university, justified by a series of events. Revisiting anti-slavery movements, Pan African and nationalistic movement, Harlem renaissance and re-orientation of African being through rewriting African historiographies. The historical part of decolonial turn is the most important aspect for theoretical foundation and hypotheses of decolonial theory in pragmatic realm. The progress of archaic consideration of decolonization influence the intellectual movement of questioning of the so called natural axioms such as racism and blackness in global lens. In order to venture in decolonizing disciplines, decolonizing the society through social movements and wars of liberation struggle sanitizes the environment of decolonizing the mind. The mechanical relationship between the environment and the mind is of utmost importance in this chapter. Social ecology and anthropological views employed to build a comprehensive expression of the sociological schema and the psychological schema in search of epistemic anatomy. In intellectual discourse, reincarnate the Memphite intellectual and Timbuktu knowledge(s) banks, issues of rewriting African history, development of African philosophy as discipline and the genesis of professional art and African literature. Notable scholars such as Cheikh Anta Diop, Kwasi Wiredu, Theophile Obenga, Molefe Kete Asante and Chinua Achebe unfolds the new historic cinema in political theatre of global society, bringing forward Afrocentric theory and decoloniality concepts. Re-engagement in the history of the decolonization and social transformation in Transmodernity creates a comprehensive thought in the understanding of decolonization theory.

Chapter four tracing the historical developments of decolonial scholarship, on how it becomes a discipline and political movement.

The chapter titled *reflection of decolonial scholarship. Critical Thinking Perspective*

In an attempt to remap the practicality of African knowledge making and decolonizing the university. The spiritual movement of epistemic freedom constructed by various cadres from the subaltern world, to facilitate the process. Chapter five engages in empirical framework in a research paper about the issue titled *"Social Transformation; An Empirical Survey on Decolonizing the University at Midlands State University"*. In the journey to make sense of the phenomenology of decolonizing the university, an empirical research paper was put into place so as to (re)focus on the comprehension of the theory. Midlands State University is the case study, varied with numerous complexities of coloniality of the university; however some of the policies and development exists in the realm of procreating African being in the citadel of knowledge. The institution created in post-colonial Zimbabwe in the year 2000 as to answer the needy of decentralizing higher education from University of Zimbabwe. The main interesting story of the institution is that it exists in post-colonial society but colonial heritage affects it to create post-colonial citizens, since the curriculum transferred from University of Zimbabwe (former University of Rhodesia) was fashioned with Eurocentric thoughts. The colonial legacy hit the bare surface of Midlands State University curriculum that affects the knowledge making at the institutions. However, educational trajectory at the university shows the relevance of the institution in social transformation and decolonial age. Issues of researches, 'massification' of higher education, scientific development and engaging in curriculum development. This study invite the qualitative research philosophy in comprehending the practicality of decolonizing the university. However, various challenges still battle down the establishment of decolonial policy at the university, such as political affairs of the country, anti-Africanism and linguistic dominance and continuity of western epistemologies- the society is yet to be democratized and decolonized. Various recommendations are put forward so as to create a meaning, empirical concept on the issue of decolonizing the university.

For theoretical development, in comprehending the phenomenology of the decolonizing the university, the book indulges in theoretical development paradigm and the concluding chapter of the book. Chapter six; *"Redefine the Image of African being from the 'Other'-Thinking Decolonizing the University"*, focuses on rebuilding the theory and rubric analysis for understanding the theory in conceptual and practical terms. After previous chapters of empirical survey, it is noted that the road is still narrow to engage in decoloniality of knowledge hence a theory to put into being guidelines and morphology to pragmatise the phenomenon. The theory composed of Afrocentric views, issuing humanising the university and refocusing on multicultural globality theory, for it to make sense and engage in practical realms

The anatomy of decolonizing the university is an ever living substance in African universities as long as coloniality of education still prevails. To engage in oiling the engine of developmentalism theory and valorizing cultural ontologies, decolonising the university is a panacea. Contemporary thoughts promote multicultural conception, the theory of decolonizing the university; embraces other centric views in fabricating unique epistemologies.

Chapter Two:
Objectivity/Subjectivity/Coloniality of the University-Ontology of the 'Other'

"Berlin Conference of 1884 was effected through the sword and the bullet. But the night of the sword and the bullet was followed by the morning of the chalk and the blackboard. The physical violence of classroom" (Ngugi wa Thiong'o; 1986)

The manufacturing of the ontology of the other problematize the mushrooming of new thoughts in global intellectual affairs. Ontology as the branch of philosophy aim to study the meaning of social world, concepts, names and labels and how it came to exists, credits social anthropological theories in explaining the beginning of social world. Social world exists from metaphysical world as a result of human interactions and anthropogenic activities, which creates social identities, ethnicity and cultures. Hence the ontology of the 'other' (re)focusing on how African humanity lost their self to other self. Africans were victimized by the circumstances to the extent that they alienated from their own thinking, cultures and society. It is difficult for a race to be intellectually productive in the event that they had lost their selves, their soul to become an "other". The virtue of being global citizenry reduced to the concept of the subject, Africa is now a global subject, subject to the civilization of the Caucasian, subjected to think and act like them that left Africa behind in the so called modernity. Events such as Arab conquest, trans-atlantics slavery and the most catastrophic colonialism influenced the dynamic of phenomenology of philosophy in global society, through achieving aims of burying the African soul alive, to create the other, a subject to western thoughts and non-thinking objects.

Making the 'Other'; A Historical Survey

The demise of Africa, and the beginning of a new being alienated from African culture and African beliefs stepped on the shores of African soil, not as a foreigner but a native African that has become the other. This historical survey focusing on how the other has been created can be used to understand the phenomenology of decolonizing the university as a theory. Williams (1992) narrates the happening of Africa's demise, in the book *destruction of black civilization*. Focusing on the bearing of new thoughts, the continent experiences centuries of vacuum, it can be called "Africa's Dark Ages", theatricalized by Arab conquest, transatlantic slave trade, epistemicide, genocides, colonial brutality and subjugation. Frantz Fanon plays a leading role in explaining colonial conditions, since blacks were reduced to objects and the "Wretched of the Earth", their land was stolen and they became tenants in their own fatherland. In the studies of the societies, ethnic groups emerges and disappears, thousands ethnic groups in classical period disappeared as a result of natural and anthropogenic activities. In the African case, the Egyptian race that used to construct pyramids are no longer there in Egypt, diluted, some mass murdered and some were runaway to other parts of Africa to formulate powerful empires such as Mali, Dogon, Songhay, Carthage and Munhumutapa. Williams (1992) and Diop (1974) credits Arab-Invasion as the beginning of African demise and creation of a new being, conceived as native but the mind is not native. Different axioms and religious practices exported to Egypt. They are being used to worship 'Ra' (God of light), Osiris, Isis, Horus and other Egyptian gods at Memphis and Thebes begun to worship Allah, thus Islamic religion dominated since the arrival of the Arabs. This situation created a new being, a devotee of a foreign God, transmogrified the self to other self. The Roman and Greek Conquests strengthened the Arab invasion and distorted all the meaning of Egyptian life, and created the ontology of the other. The discourse of the other mummified mental creativity of African being, that created a gulf or stoppage of intellectualism from the early centuries AD up to 1900. Nearly seven hundred years of civilization vacuum (William, Ibid). The new being, fashioned and disturbed by the Greco-Arab-Romano invasion, failed to (re)invent science again. However Islamic literature and Carthagian empire began to restore the glory of African being in engaging art, civilization and literature. Formulated learning centres, Timbuktu University and Al-Qarayyiwin University as academy and learning centres (Diop, 1991). In this period some of societies in Sub-Saharan Africa continue to produce art, alphabet, and literature, architecture since their original being remain unconquered by the Arabs, Romans and Greeks. Art continues in Akan, Yoruba, and Shona societies. However the coming in of Europeans inaugurated the turning point in history, the totality of African being in all corners of the continent. Europeans came with Christian religion, converted Africans, they also came with their civilization and colonized the continent. In this regard, African was forced to ban their cultural activities and embrace European culture, and created the ontology of the other, an African without African soul. The contemporary society were affected by these issues, and the French colonization engaged in deep cultural exposition, whereby the policy of (assimilado) assimilation was enacted

> "The founder of education system in the Third Republic, was also a passionate supporter of the imperial enterprise believed in the duty of 'superior races to civilize inferior', and helped to convince his contemporaries that, If France was to remain a great country, it had to carry 'wherever it could, it's language, it's customs, it's flags, it's aim and it's genius" (Bessis, 2003; p11).

From this analytic perspective, of French system of provincialization it's culture to her colonies, this influenced the creation of the other since the policy had no artificial effect of only the colonial period; but a permanent mark to the post-colonial society. It simply explains why the West Africa and North Africa, former French colonies, have been in such condition since time immemorial, that of the creation of the 'other' . This policy implemented for the Africans to do away with their original culture, and cultural demonization and alienation. Hence there are no longer original Africans and not original French. Fanon (1963) states that, French colonial policies problematize the being in Africa, whereby coloniality of being begin to manifest in form of non-thinking objects and western imitation bourgeoisie (Maldonado-Toress, 2016). Africans forced to behave like French man, speak like them and worship their God. In this regard, the coloniality of being heralded by the coming in of colonizers whereby the ontology of the 'other' was conceived. The 'other' not an original African and also not an original European-hence the equation resulted in what is discussed here as the other. Portuguese, Germans and British also do the same in procreating the 'other'. The advent of Afro-Anglo Saxony justifies the historical taxonomy of the coloniality of being. In search of truth the ontological density of Africanity still in residues as observed by Amilcar Cabral, is explained in the next chapter. The most important issues to comprehend is the concept of coloniality of university. Sylvia Wynter introduces the concept of coloniality, as the new bearing of thoughts and development of new vocabulary and explains the praxis of what is being in the global society. How black race define themselves as 'being', the coloniality of being. Ndhlovu-Gatsheni (2013) develop the theory of matrix of coloniality as the determinant factor influencing the contemporary behaviors of the sulbaternity. Wynter (2010), develops the theory of being in psychological schema, the issue of the mind that creates the other through the manifestation of the other.

Continuity of Validation of the 'Other' Being (Construction of Imperial Eurocentric Canon of Thoughts)

The paradigm of the 'other' supported by social relevance, whereby the global cosmogonies structured with two classes, the western and the other. Africa has been provincialized by the west, relegated to the bottom by western theorists. Africa no longer exists, apart from political colonialism the coloniality of the university justifies the passion for dominance of the western world. Mignolo (2011) and Grosfoguel (2013) analyzes the theory of dominance in post-modern world, in incorporating concepts such as modernity, global coloniality of the issues of mental slavery and coloniality of global south epistemologies. The way universities structure knowledge(s) premised on Eurocentric theory as creature of colonialism, hence the expansion of western geopolitics create the ends/result of coloniality of being or creation of the 'other'. Bonaventura de Sausa Santos put forward the idea of global south epistemologies as under threat from programming and learning theories fashioned in Eurocentric approach. To buttress colonialism, coloniality of the mind proliferated as to establish a permanent mark of dominance, in the process of creating the 'other'. The Eurocentric knowledge making process, plays a pivotal role in world making that creates a Manichean misanthropy and dehumanize non-western races. Issues of Eurocentric thoughts polarize the society into two, the zone of those who are human enough and the zones of sub-human, the world provincialized. Whereby Euro-American communities regarded as scientific universal societies to be emulated by the global society. Epistemology is the branch of philosophy that specializes on the production of knowledge system, a systematic reflection of knowledge making and knowledge(s). Epistemology fabricated by human interaction, hence the knowledge system is pluriverse. According to Escobar (2018), knowledge(s) are subset of culture, differ from ethnic group to ethnic group. This issue problematize the universalization of western epistemologies in universities, which creates alienation of the Africans from their culture. African homes consist of high cultural practices, such as social relations, traditional practices and folklore learning, however all these issues were swept away by western modernity and coloniality of knowledge systems in the post-colonial Africa. Home and school become two different worlds. At home culture is practiced but at school culture is defined as barbaric, hence the school world become dominant since it is viewed as key to success at the end the 'other' created in the process.

The conflicting of knowledge(s) in two worlds, where at home the issue "I am because we are", but at school "I think therefore I am" affect creativity in the process, and the later overrides the first due to vast theories and learning perspectives supporting the "I" concept, of western thoughts. Carter G Woodson (1933) devised a theory to understand the polarization of the world in intellectual movement whereby miseducation is used as the methodology in dividing the world, supporting western thoughts and rejecting Negro thoughts for the purpose of justifying the myth of racial supremacy. Theoretical materials where fashioned in Hegelian thoughts, where Africa was regarded as a continent without history. Disciplines in African universities rooted in colonial set up and western world, hence the achievement of political independence failed to make sense in post-colonial projection. Hence the new educated Africans are alienated from African being. The teaching of Sociology, Political Science, Public Administration, Economics, History, Philosophy and Anthropology are designed in western thoughts since western countries export those disciplines with their theories in Africa to achieve the aim of geopolitical expansion. From the Archives, Placide Temples and Kwasi Wiredu redefine the African Knowledge systems as based on cosmos, I am because we are (Ubuntu), that is different from Caucasoid system based on Cartesian thought, and "I think therefore I am". In this regard comparative racial studies proves epistemic variation among races living on the earth planet. John Mbiti, Pauline Hauntondji, Theophile Obenga and Henry Odera Oruka applied the conception of ethno-philosophy approach to identify the manifestation of African epistemology. African epistemology manifest in customary beliefs, art, religion, justice system, understanding the cordial relationship of nature and human being and ontological creation, folklores, economic science and comprehensive political organization. The coming in of foreign invaders established a terminus to African knowledge systems that midwifed the birth of strange epistemologies that are parallel to African discourses. Professor Lwazi Lushaba from the University of Cape Town joined the pilgrimage of secular indigenous beliefs to decolonize the long tormented university, is of the view that

> "In order to consolidate colonization, epistemic violence was the most decisive strategy to epistemicide African knowledge systems" (Lushaba; 2017).

In this regard, *I will write what I want* zealot movement by Steve Bantu Biko (Black Consciousness), discovered that "The most important weapon of the oppressor is the mind", since the mind shelters knowledge and wisdom, so as to distort the content, disfigure and destroy the world view of natives, was the main goal of the western marauders in colonial times. Dussell (2003) and Grosfoguel (2007) propagate the discourse analysis of knowledge and racial studies, knowledge is in pluriverse not universal. In an attempt to universalize the Caucasian knowledge various tertiary institutions formed in colonial regions to raise colonial flag. Professor Molefe Kete Asante states that;

> "…..A beautiful note from a Zimbabwean studying for doctorate in London. He claims to have read my works and

to have felt quite insufficiently educated by the European system of training because it taught him little or nothing about his own culture and did not integrate his knowledge that is what he had already had, knowledge into general system of knowledge promoted by Europe. I was struck by this letter because I realized the great mental and cultural pain he must have experienced during his academic career". (Asante, 2007:p25)

The above statement explains how the other created, whereby foreign knowledge system failed to integrate itself with the developmental needs of the native land. The reason there's parallel between university and social development is the impartation and production of alienated students from their culture, making it difficult for them to lead their people towards a prosperous future. According to Sadar (2008), structural racial dominance; is structural since it is fashioned on a systematic reflection of the society and influences the point of view in large scale, from historical justification to sociological schema. Universalization of Eurocentric thoughts influence the discourse of racism through the silencing of creative knowledge, in objection of indigenous knowledge in universities. Professor Sabelo J Ndhlovu-Gatsheni penned a decolonial epistle to sacred knowledge banks of Africa, and universities (Epistemic Freedom in Africa; Deprovincialisation and Decolonization), narrating the preface of epistemic violence designed to overthrow African knowledge system through transplant education and Judeo-Christian religion. In 1827 Fourah Bay College the then University of Sierra Leone was formed as university college of Durham University, Yaba College the then Ibadan University was formed in 1948 and other universities were formed as affiliate colleges of universities in Europe. Against this background, it is clear that the teaching methodology was wholly Eurocentric, that established an epistemic hegemony by the west to the rest of African continent. Africa was demised as epistemic global competitors to global spectator in the intellectual field. Molefe Kete Asante revealed by the gods of his ancestors, wrote a spiritual work about Afrocentric theory, based on total assertion of African Agency, sharing the wise worlds within black races in 2007

> "I think that intellectual project of Eurocentric hagemonists continues the objective of domination established in the earliest days of western social theory as collorary to political and economic imperialism" (Asante, 2007. P138, an Afrocentric Manifesto).

He (Asante) clarifies the objective of Eurocentric, premised on the theory of international realism founded by Niccollo Machiavelli and Hans Morgenthau based on the assertive thought of politics as struggle for power and dominance in the international system. For the West to continue domination, Eurocentric was perpetuated as universalized in colonial and post-colonial episodes. Revaluing the colonial and post-colonial educational knowledge system, it is discovered that chances of re-asserting African Agency are slim due to the dominance of Caucasoid knowledge(s). The effects of epistemic violence, affects the inner core of African minds, manifest itself outwardly whereby Africans are no longer self but other self. Africa witnesses the death of African existence, current university education alienates us from the roots. Mbembe (2016) and Nelson

Maldonado-Torres (2016) argues that, universalisation of European ideologies in all spheres of global life invites a problematic issue to knowledge(s) that led to coloniality of knowledge. After the establishment of transplant institutions, epistemic violence continued by, coloniality of knowledge perpetuated in academic space. Ama Mazama (2003) offer an apologetic statement about misconfiguration of the meaning and anthropological effects of colonization in the so called era of decolonization. This state of events, distort the meaning of independence in Africa, epistemic violence as an undiscovered residue of colonization affect the hopes of African optimism to development. Tracing African political philosophy, only Steve Bantu Biko and Edward Blyden discovers the catastrophe in the fullest context that reserves an apology to the first wave of decolonization. It is a pity to imagine the number of graduates in African universities since inceptions, as degree holders without African epistemology(s).

The Question of Language(s) and Europhonism

Europhonic expressions in Africa, send African languages to abyss and relegated them to the bottom of global economy of linguistic glory. Europhonism is the word coined by Ngugi wa Thiongo explaining the coming of western languages and imposed in Africa through colonialism and post-colonial coloniality. Unpacking the post-colonial realities of the holy citadels of African knowledge(s), the scroll of epistle extends from epistemic violence to 'linguisticides'. The main thrust of this section is to understand the discourse of indigenous languages and how it has been linguisticide in learning systems. On a mission to explore what went wrong to African indigenous issues, language capture the minds of modern post-colonial theorist. In the process of epistemic violence, linguisticides also oil the engine to trigger the process of confession and conversions at the holy altars of African academics and create the other. African languages grouped in various categories namely Semitic, Bantu and Hermitic extend to cover approximately million spoken languages across the continent (Mazrui, 1986). Ngugi Wa Thiongo in his book *Decolonising the Mind; Politics of Language in African Literature*, stresses the point of demise Africanity in literature horizon. Since language is the subset of culture, the demise of it means the demise of culture. Post-colonial tertiary education system largely encourages development of foreign languages.

> "The biggest weapon yielded and actually daily unleashed by imperialism against that collective defiance is the cultural bomb. The effect of cultural bomb is to annihilate a people's belief in their names, in their languages, in their environment, in their heritage of struggle, in their unity, in their capacities and ultimately in themselves. It makes them see the past as wasteland of non-achievement and it makes them want to distance themselves; for instance, with other people's languages rather than their own" (Ngugi wa Thiongo, 1986;3).

Linguistic imperialism, according to Ngugi wa Thiongo resulted in the creation of the 'other' being; a being that failed to appreciate his or her language or past historiography. The European mono-linguistics agenda, overrides the multilingual policies in the university education (Canagaragjah, 2007). Ngugi presents the phenomenological arguments of language governance experience in

Africa and proposes the (re)blending of independence through decolonizing the language. Presenting the arguments presented at Makerere University in 1962 (Anglonormativity, 2017), *A Conference of African Writers of English Expression*, African writers such as Chinua Achebe, Wole Soyinka and among others argue that it is high time to accept English language for relative purpose, it help us to tell our stories. The conference also justified by Professor Charles Tembo states that, "English language mutated into multiplicity of versions, African versions", which justify the worthfulness of using the language as medium of communication. The language policy in learning system promotes foreign European languages, however those languages are ecumenical according to Ali Mazrui, they have no cultural bearings like communalist languages such as ChiShona, Chichewa, Igbo, Hausa, IsiZulu. Writers such as Wole Soyinka and Leopold Senghor won Literature bureau prizes for developing European languages in literature. The multicultural heritage as the treasure of post-colonial Africa accept the use of other global languages for academic and communication process. However the language policy remains colonial since indigenous languages are subsidized, that foretells the future demise of African languages. According to Kwasi Kwa Prah, indigenous languages are only studied by those who are reading BA African Languages, MA African Languages and PhD African Languages, that restrict only one department to venture in the development of indigenous language diction and literature. The development of indigenous language is at stake, language policy is still colonial, that is tantamount to the meaning of independence to Africans.

The ontological density of Africanity consumed by Eurocentric hegemonic manifestation. Alamin Mazrui and Ali Mazrui penned book titled *"Power of Babel. Language and Governance Experience in Africa"* produce a narrative account of the situational context of African languages. The post-colonial language planning and policy of the colonizer helps it to develop. Noam Chomsky (2006) stresses the importance of language in social realism and dominance, the concept of linguistic imperialism perpetuates dominance and hinder creativity. The art of African agency in tertiary education wrestled down by linguistic imperialism, for Zeleza (2009), French, Spanish, Portuguese and English dominate the cosmology of writing and learning in Africa, and hence in this situation it is rather difficult to claim that we are independent. Frantz Fanon scriptures of nationalism of Martinique and Africa, credit the aspect of language in problematizing nationalism, in the objective of total independence. Rethinking the notion of Independence in Africa remain subtle and literary valueless due to post-colonial situation. Few writers care about African Indigenous languages; hence one is wondering when will African languages develop as global competitive languages. The analogies of China, Turkey and Japan engage in linguistic conscientization, urge every foreigner to learn their language for a certain period of time. The Asiatic and Eastern Europe language policy promote the development of vocabulary of their languages. However more focusing on European languages fed the process of Africa demise, and ties the African soul with heavy fetters and chains of Eurocentrism.

Middleman in the process of making the "other"-being.

Middleman or agents play a pivotal role in the implementation of the coloniality of being and making the 'other' in academic world. Most lecturers and professors still do not realize the mental effects of exposing and recommending students to focus largely on Eurocentric theories in academic arguments and research. Independence remain unfinished in post-colonial Africa, which create a problem in defining the word post-colony? Since post-colony in literary perspective focused on the conception of the era of being free and post-colonial era. How do we define Africa as a post-colony? We are still subalterns, and colonialism continues. Eurocentric administrators are in charge of every sphere of life, mainly, university education. During Africanization of industrial sector in early years of post-independence Africa, the academic sector remained European. Molefe Kete Asante narrates a teleological conception of colonialism treated as economic and political problem, hiding its contribution to confusions, that remained the problematic phenomenon to the re-assertion of African Agency. Carter Woodson (1933) wrote *the Miseducation of Negroes in America,* this story transcend to the African discourse whereby miseducation exist since time immemorial in Africa. The holy citadels of knowledge, heretic knowledge has been preached and propagated by Apostles of Eurocentric, the so called administrators. Tracing historical events, the establishment of transplant universities in post-colonial Africa exported western values to the epistemic trade ports of Africa. Transplant universities, fashioned by external administration, disciplines, their learning methods were highly European. For Instance the discipline of philosophy rejects African philosophy in colonial period as it was testified by Kwasi Wiredu. Social science and humanities disciplines still exist and is taught in Eurocentric thought. The coloniality of administration affect the conception of curriculum development and exploration of knowledge banks in comparative studies. The coming in of transplant universities, European professors administered university colleges in Africa, and established the legacy of Eurocentric thoughts. Historical and theoretical books printed in Europe, written by European scholars that led to the distortion of African issues, for instance writers such as D. N Beach and J.B Cobbings distorted African historiographies, perpetuated the writings of Levy Brahl and David Hume that Africa is a continent without historical conscience; the historical existence of Africa is largely barbarous.

Conclusion

The strength of western being influence the demise of African being. African being lost meaning in the discourse of global society, since it transmogrified itself from original African self and emulates western way of life which creates the 'other' being that is far too to be European being. The other revolved in between, African metaphysics and western ontological being, hence that kind of being has little capabilities in producing knowledge towards progressive theory. The historical taxonomy of making of the 'other' explained from historical point of view of Arab conquest that created more than seven hundred years of little intellectual progress. Colonization, furthered the process of coloniality of the being and programmed the discourse of inferiority beliefs of the black through exposure to western knowledge(s) in colonial universities. The disciplines, in search for truth about sociological, political, psychological and philosophical issues of African society affected the justification of western 'opinions' as truth in knowledge production, and resulted in the perpetuation of mental slavery and alienation. The legacy of western being to procreate the 'other', a poor being that cannot produce knowledge. However this is not a natural axiom, fabricated by the legacy of the west to continue dominance in polarised society.

Chapter Three:
Historical Materialism of the Decolonial-turn-liberate African intellectualism

Epistemic freedom is the cardinal principle of decolonizing the university. Decolonization of the university means total re-assertion of African knowledge freedoms, mummify and cement colonial residues in former colonies, and also establish a polycentric template of knowledges. It began as nationalistic movement in Ghana and a guerrilla movement in Mozambique, Kenya and Zimbabwe. This historical analogy drove us back to Ama Mazama and Molefe Kete Asante review on misconfiguration of the effects of colonization, the maltreatment of colonialism by nationalists left catastrophic residues, coloniality of education. The brilliance of Kwame Nkrumah, Julius Nyerere and other nationalist failed to diagnose the problematic expression of colonialism to the state of mind and education. Mbembe (2016) define decolonization of education as the shift of thinking from the myth of universality of western knowledge(s) to embrace African agency in learning system. Since Professor Achilles Mbembe narrowly focuses on Africa, Ramon Grosfoguel and Walter D Mignolo offer a universal analysis of the concept of decolonization of education as the re-assertion of multi-racial knowledge(s) to academic issues. The main objective of epistemic decolonization is to correct ills of the past, rewriting African historiography and reclaiming African epistemology. According to Maldonado-Torres (2016), coloniality as a concept and social movement, is aimed to detoxicate the toxic substances imposed on global south by the so called great powers in global politics. It include social activism. The intellectual heritage of global south based on myth and beliefs has been railed off by the so called global modernity, social and intellectual movement engages in the battle to restore the dignity of decentered ontologies and axiologies.

Deconstructing the Ecology and Political Space

What is ecology? In this chapter it's not about geographical issue, but it's a political space or social environment whereby humans beings dwell on and establish social relations. Deconstructing ecology is more important since it acts as a clean-up campaign of the environment to be habitable and enable ideas to form, ideas of dismantling colonial legacies and coloniality. The story has its roots in anti-colonial resistance of Queen Nyabingah in Ethiopia, Queen Nzinga in Congo and Nehanda in Zimbabwe and anti-slavery movements in the Caribbean cartographies. The beginning of Anti-Slavery campaign in Europe and America championed by William Wilberforce heralded a new turning point of history and new world thoughts. The anti-slavery movement midwifes the new thinking in black communities, by beginning to question and theorizing the existing myth about the society. All societal beliefs, concepts and existing literature questioned and deconstructed issues of identity, gender, racism and political civilization among black communities. Afro-American nationalism influenced the Liberian state project of back to Africa by Marcus Garvey by engaging in decolonizing the society. Marcus Garvey influence radical social transformation in the Caribbean and USA, whereby Black Nationalism or blackness venturism was an exerting pressure against the dominant issue of slavery and racial cosmogonies in global society. The subalterns' movement shuttered the dream of white supremacism, which began to fall apart, as it failed to hold the anarchy exerted by Black Nationalism. Pan Africanism movement also influenced the movement of decolonization in the African society. Martin (2003) defines Pan Africanism as the movement aimed to rebut African inferiority and restore African glory on the issue of land and identity. Africans abroad and Africans in Africa engages in civic movement that put pressure and threatens western ideologies since decolonization remain unpredictable in African soil. The morphology of Black Nationalism in Africa and diaspora influenced by George Padmore, Frantz Fanon, Edward Blyden, William DuBois, Sekoure Toure, Kwame Nkrumah, Martin Luther King Jnr and Malcom X changed the society to engage in political movement as an option to dismantle the long dominating political imperialism. Civil rights movements in the USA, the War of liberation struggle in Lusophone and Anglophone Africa, and constitutional arrangements and independence in Africa influenced the background of decolonizing the education in global south institutions. In 1957 Ghana gained independence that created a turning point in history of humanity, whereby a number of African states followed suit, by 1994 the continent defeated apartheid and colonization that showed a successful movement of African nationalism. However the journey was still there, independence was a superficial one, not an absolute that promoted the existence of Hannah Arendt theory of emptiness-no longer political colonialism and not yet independence. In the phenomenology of decolonizing the university, various intellectual development across the continent and abroad ushered in a new dispensation of decolonial turn in academic affairs.

Historical Taxonomy of African (Black) Intellectual Movement.

By transcending to the decolonization movement, the environment has been a safe place, that influenced the pressure of subconciousness to determine consciousness of the society. The relationship between the environment and decolonization of the university is of importance, since the environment determines human behavior or human behavior creates the environment. Decolonial environment and independent African governance system influences the needy for Africanizing the university hence decolonizing of the westernized universities. Human behavior of decolonized minds and social activism influences the struggle for deconstructing the dominant ontologies and re-orientation of African being and the university education. Mignolo (2003) states that the historical transformation of the recognition of the knowledge(s) of the historically marginalized people, Caribbeans and Africans, displays a new thought of social structure and knowledge-making politics.

Transmodernity is as an event, system and ideology that influences all facets of life and questions the metaphysical nature of the society, such as issues of racism. Started in the USA Harlem renaissance, it influenced the intellectuals movement in 1912 since it was aimed at creating Afro-American art with African cultures, and promote black poetry, art and literature. Theorizing and questioning European art, the myth of blacks as people without intelligentsia and that cannot produce literature was dismantled through the influence of Harlem renaissance whereby slavery become the main theme that influenced African-American Literature. Fredrich Douglas' world read slavery experience story, kick-started the movement of African art, poetry and literature. The metaphysical locality of Afro-American Literature and Art influenced the slave trade as the most important event in the history of Afro-Americans. In this regard, new thoughts developed about the black nation, and influenced academic nationalism as to reconstruct the glory of African-Americans.

According to Giyatri Spivak (2010), the rise of subalterns voices in political affairs of the globe begun to midwife new theories and publications about the society. Carter G Woodson (1933) analysis of *Miseducation of the Negroes* developed the zeal to repatriate on the so called real concept of decolonizing the university. Woodson narrate the issue of how Negroes were miseducated, they were programmed on certain theories that were designed to promote white supremacism and curve black inferiority.

> "At a Negro summer school two years ago, white instructor gave course on the Negro, using for his text a work which teaches that whites are superior to the blacks. When asked by the students why he used such text book the instructor replied that he wanted them to get that point of view. Even schools for Negroes, then, are places where they must be convinced of their inferiority. The thought of inferiority of the Negro is drilled into him in almost every book he studies. If he happens to leave school after he masters the fundamentals, before he finishes high school or reaches college, he will naturally escape some of this bias and may

recover in time to be of service to his people" (Woodson, 1933; p2).

Carter G Woodson narrate and exhibit the discourse of miseducation, whereby the view referred by the instructors is the theory of black primitivity and inferiority, blending the white supremacist theory in education. However questioning remain the solution in breaking the yoke designed by the imperialist to perpetuate their beliefs and natural cultures in sociological manifestation. The disjuncture between education and Negro life development shows a sorry case. Carter Woodson as a creature of Harlem Renaissance creates a new turning point in the history of Negroes, which influence the superb writings from scholars such as Dr George G.M James. Dr George James in 1954 completed a historical project about the origins of Greek Philosophy in African perspective. Since universities are communities of scholars and students searching for truth it happened at the Arkansas University, from Woodson class descriptions of a student and instructor, influencing the research project about questioning the foundation and meaning of Greek Philosophy (Clarke 1998). The book credit Egyptian philosophy as founding the thoughts of world civilization and Greek Philosophy in analyzing the Greek philosophy's historical incompleteness. The book titled *"Stolen Legacy; The Egyptian Origins of Greek Philosophy" published in 1954* elucidate how Egyptian philosophy was stolen into Greek philosophy that problematized thoughts and history from antiquity to present generation.

"It is a mere prejudice to believe that the philosophical epoch of humanity begins first among Greeks in the fifth century BC. This prejudice implies that other ancient people did not engage in speculative thought transcending experience, but it always attempts to explain, interpret, and unifies it in order to systematize it. Speculative thought, using aphorisms, allusions, metaphors, negative or positive methods, and dialectics, can be oral or written, and it is necessarily connected with the problems of life. Thus philosophy can be defined as systematic reflective thinking of life" (Yu-Lan 1976; p16)

This philosophical reflection of the people of the past and knowledge making, credits Dr James historical project of redefining the birth of Greek philosophy as a creature of Egyptian philosophy, later referred to as mystery by the western philosophers. The incapacity of black people to produce literature and philosophy has been examined in the historic intellectualism of the ancient Egypt. The black empire without borders, should exist in large landmasses dividing the oceans of the world, realizing our nationality, form a nation beyond boarders and form a movement against the so called white superiority, an intellectual movement. Transforming the sociological schema designed to dehumanize black people intellectual movement in rewriting the phenomenon of Kemetic civilization by George James inaugurates the new thought and influences the new thinking in history and philosophy. However this kind of text failed to venture in academic space and was relegated to the periphery in the libraries of African Studies, kept confidential by the owners of universities, the white race threatened by this kind of scholarship. The movement of black studies in United States of America marks the genesis of the need to decolonize the university. Black studies movement designed its objective in the prism of creating education with production to black communities and to learn African cultures and history. Woodson (Ibid) review the miseducation of the Negroes whereby there are not exposed to the history of Negroes, and some of the history written by the white people with racial interests and largely biased, in order to rebut the programming of such theories the introduction of black studies is an alternative. As the creature of Harlem Renaissance, Hispanophone, Caribbean Lusophone and Anglophones Negroes in American continent engages in cultural nationalism in influencing education system to accept the pure and true history of the Black society. Harlem renaissance as continual event manages to create new identities of justifying the rights of blacks as part of American history and American hemisphere through introducing the Term 'Afroamerica'. Julio Le Riverend (re)conceptualize a hemisphere "Afroamerica" defined as black zone situated basically on the two atlantics coasts of the two continents, Augustin Lao-Montes calls for notion of Afroamerica that encompasses black experiences (Slavery and Racism) throughout Americas. Afro-Americanism defines a metaphysical relations of the black community and American hemisphere. The term was coined to the meaning of the African identity in Diaspora cartography, since values the roots in integrating the words 'Afro'-'America' defines a black empire of the African descent. The issue continues to establish the African-American Studies as an interdisciplinary studies to study the critical issues of Negro race, history, culture, identity, art, science and philosophy (Clarke 1998). This intellectual development ventures into the liberation of epistemologies of the South and dismantling mental slavery academic studies. African-American Studies as a discipline started using various literature publication about racial issues and slavery already published, however it engaged in literature revolution and reorient the system in black discourses.

Temple University developed the scope and theory of African-American Studies (Abdul Alkallmat) as disciplines, renaming it to Africology, an interdisciplinary aiming to study African American and African issues in Afrocentric perspective (Karenga 1994). It managed to integrate the two in intellectual realm so as to redefine the black empire, an empire without borders. Molefe Kete Asante (1991, 2003, 2007 and 2016) manage to develop the discipline that begins the journey of decolonizing the university, comprehending the thoughts behind the Africology disciplines. I will write what I want editorial series by Bantu Steve Biko influenced the conception of epistemic freedom through the mantra of Black Consciousness. The integration of black identity and issues of the mind procreates a new movement that focused on deconstructing the mind.

In Biko observation, the mind was the most potent weapon used by the enemy, they influenced the thinking and theorizing in every facets of life by programming creation ontologies through the policy of Apartheid. In an attempt to divide the race, dehumanize black people by denying them their existence as global competitive race. Like Franz Fanon and Steve Biko intellectual movement mainly revolves in the objective of deconstructing the mind, that explains Woodson (Ibid) view of the process of convincing blacks about their inferiority and a race without civilization. Amilcar Cabral put forward the idea of culture as the most important weapon that raise awareness and Black Nationalism against colonialism, hence deconstructing the mind, refocusing on thinking the indigenous cultural movement. Biko theory exhibit itself in dichotomy, as intellectual movement and political movement and inaugurates the genesis of the need for decolonizing the university to bury the alienation catastrophe resultant from learning disciplines embroidered in Eurocentric approach about white race superiority, history and modes of 'being-in-the-world'. Black consciousness as the movement of the black empire, the oppressed people and subalterns, according to Biko's definition of black empire, introduces issue of thinking, questioning and theorizing the dominant policies and problems about the race. South Africa Student Organization (SASO/AZAPO) existed, it comprised of the masse opinion and Biko's objective of deconstructing the mind in learning institution. The organization redefine university as a centre of scholars searching for truth and Africans need to understand the meaning of university in African perspective. As not only an institution for having social status but promote the development of Black race through introducing courses and societies that discusses about black issues in South Africa and the world at large.

The ontology of blackness as synonym of subalterns and questioned in black consciousness from natural pretension to artificial outlook helped the success of Black Consciousness Intellectual Movement. In historic materialism of Decolonial Turn, Steve Biko social evaluation proved futile in the genesis of the meaningful social movement and transformation on deconstructing the mind about the values inserted by the white race to African students that resulted in grave catastrophe and alienation of students from their culture and society. Most of the contemporary movements against colonial curriculum, in South Africa are held in memory of Steve Bantu Biko. The era of African nationalism midwifes issues of decolonial movement, whereby various scholars began the journey of freeing the minds from colonial subjugation. What has been explained about Levy Brahl and Fredrich Hegel about Africa, as a continent without historical conscience has been questioned during the period of early nationalism to post-colonialism, through the growth of various Intellectuals in the continent, academic issues were questioned. The dominant thoughts for over two centuries led to numerous publication about Africa as Dark Continent and approaching it's permanency in academic, shaped the world sociogenic structure and even the black race, and subalterns were convinced to accept the view. Social science teaching methodology unspares those arguments since a number of theories begun to be criticized that threatened the position of white race superiority in knowledge banks and academic spaces. In search for truth, the origins and reason of some white supremacist theories questioned such issues of religion, culture, civilization and philosophy that produced an array of thoughts in academic world.

Struggle to justify the theory; opposing schools of thoughts emerged with social and scientific evidence to prove their thoughts that create a turning point of thoughts in human history. Every race has history, history of glory and downfall, these thoughts influenced the questioning existing in texts that explain African history as only barbaric and history of downfall, and in other issues it cannot be called history since there was no any documentation. The misconception of African historiographies and African anthropology shows the difference between western epistemology and that of Africa, whereby in western lens there was no history but in African lens there's a great rich history of the continent which need to be studied. George James, (1954) managed to produce a material argument about the existence of African philosophy as its influence to world's thoughts. Universities in Africa, students taught about the barbaric condition of African history in colonial era, read and referenced European text that alienated them from the knowledge(s) and cultures of African being.

The question of Ancient Egypt invites many opposing arguments about race and knowledge(s), however with the help of Archaeological inventions the question of race resolved through phenomenological positivist discoveries of Ancient races of Kemet. United Nations Educational, Scientific and Cultural Organization (UNESCO) in 1974 organized a symposium that created various thoughts and theories among Egyptologist. Theophile Obenga a leading scholar in Egyptology justified the black race existence in Egyptian philosophic development. Anthropologist and Egyptologists begun the journey of correcting Eurocentric thoughts of African history to decolonize area study. Cheikh Anta Diop published many books to justify the African agents in civilization. *The Origins of African Civilization; Myth or Reality (1974), Civilization or Barbarism, An Authentic Anthropology (1981), The peopling of Ancient Egypt and Deciphering of the Meroitic Script (1997), Pre-colonial Black Africa (1998)*

The Anthropological survey of Cheikh Anta Diop provides an evidence of Africa's intellectual heritage, that begun the journey of decolonizing the area study. Cheikh Anta Diop solved the Egyptian question exceptionally, that inaugurate new thoughts and interest in research about African affairs in decolonial intellectual movement.

> "The history of Africa will remain suspended in air and cannot be written correctly until African historians dare to connect it with the history of Ancient Egypt" (Diop, 1974)

The Egyptian questions, as the centre of world's civilization, Cheikh Anta Diop express and research on the connection between Egypt and the rest of Africa, which clearly explains the justification of Black races as the father of Kemet civilization. The question of blackness is justified by various scientific methodologies of research whereby notable Egyptian philosophers were black. Developing the theory proposed by Martin Banal 'Black Athena' and George James 'Stolen Legacy', Cheikh Anta Diop corrected the historical injustices that existed in Eurocentric text that describe Africa as the continent without historical conscience (Levy Brahl). The commencement of the unraveling of the African historiography provides an impetus role to decolonize education in post-colonial societies. Ivan Van Sertima, Chancellor Williams, Josef Ben Joachanan, John Henrique Clarke and Marimba Ani joined the academic struggle to liberate academic space since vast literature publication about Africa was largely distorted and provides new themes in African studies, however Africanity historians engage in massive research, anthropological and archaeological researches that provide evidence about the glory of black race, architecture of pyramids and Great Zimbabwe and, mathematical evolutions.

> "The ancestors of the Blacks, who today live mainly in Black Africa, were the first to invent mathematics, astronomy, the calendar, sciences in general, arts, religion, agriculture, social organisations, medicine, writing, technique, architecture" (Diop 1974)

This is not a disputed argument, but supported by relevant methodologies and empirical examples from carbon dating, rock art and ancient story telling. The tales of African civilization exist in present literature that justifies the art and scientific mind of a black man. *Is there any African Philosophy?* This question occupy a historical framework to the development of the movement of decolonizing disciplines in universities. Pauline Hauntondji, John Mbiti, Kwasi Wiredu and Odera Oruka (sage philosophy) justifies the existence of African philosophy in contrast to western philosophy. Ethnophilosophy school of thought primarily focuses on ethnicity and philosophy, issues of beliefs and cultures incorporated in the discipline of philosophy to develop the scope of decolonizing the disciplines.

However professional philosophy school of thought, wedges the gap and correct the mistakes by ethno-philosophers through introducing political thoughts, the aspect of reason and cultural developments to develop African philosophy. Henry Odera Oruka invented the methodology of African philosophy research, the sage philosophy based on inquiring the wise nobleman of the society about history, epistemology, ethics, metaphysics and ontology.

> "......Philosophy departments tended not to develop the impression that there was any such thing. I graduated from the University of Ghana in 1958 after at least five years of undergraduate study. In all those years I was not once exposed to the concept of African philosophy. J. B. Danquah's *The Akan Doctrine of God*, Subtitled *A Fragment of Gold Coast Ethics,* had been published in 1945. Yet of all the information that was made available at the Department of Philosophy, that would have remained a secret to me If I

hadn't made acquaintance with it in my own private reading at secondary school". (Wiredu, 2004; p1)

Analyzing this note, Kwasi Wiredu educational account shows the role of coloniality of education in alienating Africans from their cultures and society. The issue of African philosophy remained a disputed issue in Kwasi Wiredu time, whereby European philosophy taught in African university, the continent was regarded as without philosophy. However post-colonial scholars engage in serious research and search for truth in redefining African philosophy and influence it to have space in academic disciplines. The debate about African philosophy, theology, political science to engage in research editorial as a way to achieve the goals of decolonizing disciplines. The historiography of decolonizing the university premised the genesis of publication of African literature across the continent. *Things Fall Apart* by Chinua Achebe marks the beginning of the gestation period of African literature in post-colonial Africa and facilitates decolonization of education through writing African stories, fiction and curriculum development. In comparison to phenomenology of colonial African literary studies, it was difficult for Africans to tell their stories of culture, civilization, sociogenic activities and heroic tales. Wole Soyinka and Ngugi wa Thiongo focused on theatricalising decolonizing literature through incorporating oral tradition in writing stories and trilogy of Kings and Queens of Africa. Zimbabwe novelist and poets such as Aaron Chiundura Moyo, AC Hodza, AM Hamutyinei and Patrick Chakaipa transformed oral traditional stories about the past historiographies of people of Madzimbabwe into writing manuscripts, and developed Shona poetry, literature and drama in the promotion of both indigenous language and cultural cosmology of Zimbabwe. The historical materialism of the discourse of decolonial turn inaugurated new thoughts and the need for publishing empirical and conceptual analytics about decolonizing the university and liberating intellectualism of the South.

Theoretical Taxonomy and Paradigms
Afrocentric Theory

From the issues of re-writing African history, black studies movements and academic disciplines development theatricalising the dramatic expression of the existence of Afrocentric theory, Professor Molefe Kete Asante introduced and developed Afrocentric theory to debunk Eurocentric paradigm in learning and teaching methodology.

In an attempt to decolonize the university, Afrocentric theory is a useful methodological theory in understanding and researching African history and anthropology. Afrocentric theory defined as total re-assertion of African Agency.

> "Afrocentric is therefore a consciousness quality of thought, mode of analysis, and an actionable perspective where Africans seek, from Agency, to assert subject place within the context of African history" (Asante; 2007;p16).

Professor Molefe Kete Asante clarify the concept and paradigmatic atomic exposition of Afrocentric theory to examine the subject of Africans in historical literary, architectural, ethical, philosophical, economic and political life. He wrote the book titled *Cheikh Anta Diop; An Intellectual Portrait* in 2006 as to honor the contribution by Dr

Cheikh Anta Diop to the development of Afrocentric theory as the research theoretical paradigm on African issues. Maurena Karenga, Theophile Obenga, Ama Mazama, Cheikh Anta Diop staged as the main characters in the development of Afrocentric theory in the objective to rethink disciplines and university. As it is symbolled by Sankofa bird, it is aimed to remember the dismembered that creates a large expanse to decolonize the university. Revisiting Mazrui (1984), Mahomva (2014), Ndhlovu-Gatsheni (2013) and Mandani (2004) nature of analysis, it creates the development of Africanity paradigm as the object in African phenomenology. Early etal (1994) argue that, Afrocentric as an academic assortment, therefore, serves the purpose of binding together the various elements of African and African-American studies, transforming them to an interdisciplinary assortment unified into a discipline, with ideological and intellectual goals, political purpose, and a set of commonly understood methods and theories.

> "Afrocentric seeks to examine every aspect of the subject place of Africans in historical, literary, architectural, ethical, philosophical, economic, and political life"(Ibid;p17)

Molefe Kete Asante went on to explain the concept and feasibility of Afrocentric approach in paradigmatic aspect. According to Mazama (2003), Afrocentric is not only a mere world view, but rather it is a paradigm that results in the (re)thinking of social and historical reality of African people. Afrocentric, an intellectual paradigm, takes no authority to prescribe anything, neither a religion or belief system; it is a paradigm that suggests all discourse about African people should be grounded in centrality of Africans on their own narrative.

Afrocentric paradigm employ a shift of new thinking in narrating African stories using African agency, that proves the theory is useful in the phenomenology of decolonizing the university since it is Afro-centeredness. Afrocentric theory engages in humanization of the university through the introduction of Africology, African-American Studies, African Studies and African History disciplines fashioned by Afrocentric thought and model. Afrocentric paradigm as the methodology in developing unique social science and humanities has been applied that also led to the development of Pan Africanism as academic ideology. However Afrocentric theory is not an ethno-valorized aspect that degrades other centric view like the nature of Eurocentric and not merely a world view but rather a paradigm that results in the reconceptualization of the social and historical reality of African people, in a multicultural heritage to explore global epistemic cosmology. In nutshell, Afrocentric theory suggest all discourse about African people is grounded in the centrality of African's own narrative to champion decolonizing the university.

Epistemic Freedom/Decoloniality of Thoughts

Similar to other theories, the atomic composition of decoloniality theory maintains the circus of shifting of believers and conceptual phenomenon to ethno-centered approach. In reclamation of African epistemology, Nelson Maldonado Torres (2016) introduced the trichotomy approach to the understanding of the atoms of the decoloniality theory, mandated to provide a framework to corrode mental slavery.

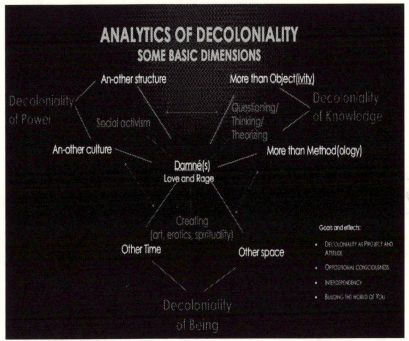

Source; *Maldonado Torres, "Outline Ten Theses of Decoloniality and Colonialty"*

This diagram, explain the composition of decoloniality theory in paradigmatic conception. Decoloniality of power, mainly decolonize the university administration based on the concept of social activism as to create an other-structure, this is justified by decolonizing the university movements in South Africa, theatricalized by *Rhodes Must Fall* demonstrations. Social activism owe methodological approach in decolonizing the university administration, black studies movement in the US creates an analogous influence to the events aimed to debunk the miseducation of Africa. Revisiting historical roots of decolonial movement, social activism remain a trustworthy methodology to regain the lost ontologies. As it is proven by history, Harlem renaissance, Pan African movements and various social activisms that yield independence. Amilcar Cabral, Steve Biko, Julius Nyerere, Robert Mugabe and other nationalist leaders adopted the method and yielded results, of independence and self-ruling. In this regard, the recent South African Student activism held in memory of Steve Biko proved useful in midwifing the system of decolonizing the university as intellectual and cultural movement. The being has been colonized, humanising the university through art, love and spiritual movement of the identity group, normally the black race engineers the growth of nationalism aimed to decolonize the being.

Spiritual movement is an objective to unite the subalterns to engage in nationalistic mass movement. Questioning, Thinking and Theorizing act as the corner stone and methodology to decolonize the object, the university. This has been epitomized by the creation of African literature, rewriting African history, introducing new paradigms such as Afrocentric in remembering the dismembered. Triple dimension theory developed by Nelson Maldonado Torres emerges victorious in analyzing the issues of decoloniality in the objective to create African being

Conclusion

In a nutshell, questioning of terminologies and associating epistemologies over the terms of blackness led to the rise of (re)conceptualizations of new thoughts in philosophy and social science discipline. Tracing the quintessence of the beginning of social transformation mainly in intellectual realm was influenced by the anti-slavery movement. As it is highlighted in this chapter, anti-slavery movement influenced by the recognition and rethinking of black people as equal to white races than it has been taught, hence then have revolved until slavery was abolished. The abolishment of slavery created a new turning point in history but left the work unfinished, since mental slavery continued through racism and existence of programming policies still to justify white superiority. Harlem renaissance came as redemptive strategy to bury the residues of slavery through formulating black art, literature and writings. Various scholarships appear to finish the job, George James, Steve Biko and Cheikh Anta Diop to mention a few developed the new thoughts of African history through dismantling the Hegelian legacy. Decolonizing the university was conceived after a series of events and developments, such as Cheikh Anta Diop project of rewriting African history, Rhodes Must Fall and Fees Must Fall in South Africa.

Chapter Four:
Reflections of Decolonial Scholarship; A Critical Thinking Perspective

The previous chapter borrow Karl Marx jargons of historical materialism as the best explanation on the historical development of decolonial theory. The essay shifts from traditional understanding of historical materialism as a discourse of change, class struggle and revolution to a discourse that define the materiality of sublime historical movement of questioning the existing traditions of knowledges in the academic society. In this regard, the meaning of the historical materials in this collection of essays is referring to the decolonial movement as a resource, a tangible material to bank on to justify the argument of the possibilities of epistemic freedom. The aim of this essay is to provide an enlightenment of what decoloniality is? From different metaphysical locations and connect it with the previous essay for better understanding of the struggle. The important issue of the decolonial scholarship, is to reflect its weaknesses by its ontological existence in academics only, provides literature through countless books, monographs and countless journal articles but failed to influence practical change and realities in the societies. The main purposes of academics or universities is to provide social change, hence it is stagnant to academic papers and theoretical knowledges with less practical relevance- that is the main themes of this whole collections of essays, to demonstrates and suggest the practical movement for decolonial change. This chapter, provides existing literary analysis, debates and major themes of the theory to creates fertile ground for practical magnum of this discourse.

Deconstructionism or Decoloniality? Luso-Hispanic Paradigm

Professor Ama Mazama, a distinguished Afrocentric-linguist define paradigm as the theory that consist of the relationship between a critical thinking and the anthromorphic interaction as to pontificate problem, tenets and problems within the tentacles of the society. In this regard, the society is a laboratory of humanist and social scientist whereby they diagnosis a problem and develop a certain theory for pragmatic reasons and social change. Given this situation, the problem is coloniality of epistemologies, and decolonial scholars provides prescriptions on how to cure this disease for the better of the society and promote epistemic freedom. Prior to the major theme of discussion of this section, a historical analysis is very necessary and led us on the journey of comprehending Decoloniality as theory and practice. This section purported to develop a new critical thinking, but not in a closet form, the Luso-Hispanic world is used a case study theme to understand the meaning of the discourse and its existentiality as a social phenomenon. Clarke (1998) and Joachanan (1996) provides a key understanding of the social problem developed historically that later conceived the rise of decolonial and deconstructionist project in the region. Christopher Columbus as the great man in history of conquest and exploration is known by his murderous legacy of discovering America and dehumanize the native Indians in the region.

The famous Valladolid judgment, rescue native Americans, since others say they are people without soul, to legitimize slavery, however the other side we say they are people with soul due to their color and easy conversion to Christianity, hence Pope's rule in favor of La Casas who supports the existence of soul in those natives. This famous judgment, necessitates transatlantic slave trade, when blacks viewed as people without soul in Hegel historical philosophy, and justifiable in Western religious aspects (Grosfoguel 2007). This story gives a different aspect of decolonial scholarship in the Caribbean world, the slave rebellion in Haiti and the concern for resisting European captivity develops a unison schema among oppressed groups. The deconstructionism, influenced by critical thinking paradigm from Jürgen Habermas, Marx Hokheimer and Theodor Ardono from Frankfurt School of thought, challenge the existing structure of the society and the imperial being (Dussel 1994). Post-structural scholars such as Michael Foucault, Jacques Derrida, Judith Butler, Marx Althuser provides a version of understanding of the oppressed individuals, whereby the systems, structures and so called world values creates subjects and limits the freedoms of the people. The notion of Punishment, Prison, Epistemology, Government, Culture and Cosmologies are designed in a way to degrade human beings, as well as to make them subjective to the demands of popular structures. In doing so, the theory of post-structuralism, critical thinking and deconstructioning projects influences the growing trends of decolonial scholarship in the Caribbean. Sylvia Wynter coin the term 'coloniality' to explain the conditions of the effects of Eurocentric modernity to the ones who were once denied humanity. The condition is unbearable, whereby the former colonized societies were dehumanized, and this continue in form of racism hence 'coloniality' (Wynter 1994). Systematic racism/patriarchal/coloniality-imperial designed world provides a realization to challenge the discourse of globalization and the so called western modernity, the western modernity viewed as only truthful world view and way of life and imposed violently to the global margins.

> "One of the most powerful myths of the twentieth century was the notion that the elimination of colonial administrations amounted to the myth of 'post-colonial' world. The heterogeneous and multiple global structures put in place over a period of 450 years did not evaporate with juridical-political decolonization of the periphery over past 50 years. We continue to live under the same 'colonial power matrix' with juridical-political decolonization we moved from a period of global coloniaty" (Grosfoguel 2007; 2019)

From Ramon Grosfoguel, this existing global structure based on coloniality of being, hidden in the armpits of modernity and globalization, realized and challenged by the authors and scholars. The challenge was not just academic, but political. Mignolo (2013) plays a most important role in fabricating decolonial epistemology from the global South, through exposing the darker side of western modernity. Western modernity is a complex social issue, whereby it promotes misdefinition of other cultures, universalize the Eurocentric notion of truth, patriarchal, promotes racism, capitalism, presenting the coloniality of human rights and even continue the deleterious of mental confusion, epistemicide. The darker Side of western modernity, came into being as analytical book of the condition of the global south, the idea influenced by the writings of Enrique Dussel (1971) (philosophy of liberation), and Boarder thinking by Gloria Anzaldua (1983). It explains the conditions and realities of dehumanization and depernolization of global south into demne's (Fanon 1968 and Maldonado-Toress 2007). The suggested ways is to engage in 'boarder thinking' or promote the thinking within the sororities of the dehumanized population, challenge the Eurocentric paradigm, not in a deconstructionist project but in a transmodernity, go beyond the idea of deconstruction. From the far south hemisphere, Linda Tuhwai Smith, popularizes the idea of decolonizing research methodologies on Indigenous population (Smith 2018).

This radical penetration of decolonial idea into researches informed by the existing research works under Eurocentric theoretical frameworks and methodologies that even distorts truth of an indigenous being. The structure of anthropology and ethnographic researches are purely Eurocentric in nature, and even failed to represent better facts of the indigenous population hence the call for decolonizing methodologies was an avid interest in debunking Eurocentric cannon of thoughts. Reaewyn Connell, also develops a southern theory, put more emphasis on reconstructing the global south epistemologies in global economy of knowledge.

Decolonize Public Intellectual Space-African Voices

"Is another world therefore possible?. African side, it is clear that another world cannot be possible as long as the continent and its people are not fully decolonized and the snares of the post-colonial neo-colonized world not broken.

This will require an epistemic rebellion that enabling the re-imagine another world free from western tutelage and African dictators that enjoy western values (Ndhlovu-Gatsheni 2013, pp263-264)

What another world? Unlike decolonial scholars from the Hispanic society, African epistemic movement projects themed on recreating another space, another world since their (African) world was obliterated in the public sphere by colonialism. The main theme is to remove the existence of Europe in African cartography, since the way of life, meditation and even dreaming was Europeanized by the forces of colonialism. In this regard, the issue of African image distorted, African aesthetic and the way of thinking also largely distorted through colonial aggressive treatment to the existence of African-hood. Ndhlovu-Gatsheni (2013) make it clear that the non-existence of the people (Africans) and the continent(Africa) premised on the early Afro-European contact in post-Berlin society. Do Africans Exist? This is not just a rhetoric question, but a logical one as it seeks to comprehend the discourse of Africanity, African consciousness among the so called Africans. What is to be African? (Mudimbe 2001, Gatsheni 2013) coin the view that, the historical situation of colonialism and slave trade construct African identities, hence in so doing there's the absence of Africaness among African, since that slavery was not just a physical one but go beyond to determine the thinking in the grey matters of the African person, colonialism was just a physical, an ideographic event, but it also wrestles down the ontological prognosis of Afrocentric thinking, values and way of life. Hence in search of existence of Africans challenge intellectuals to provide better solution of recreating African public image, re-establish Africa in the atlas of world humanity.

The creation of another world, facilitated by epistemic rebellion, which means to violently fight against the existing canon of thoughts that degrades Africans, and omit the glory of African stories in the pages of public intellectual development. African decolonial scholars focusing on constructing the canon of thoughts that are metaphysically in nature and re-centering African world view in academic affairs and the way of thinking. Afro-American Scholars such as Professor John Henrick Clarke, John G Jackson, Josef Ben-Joachanan and Professor Ivan Van Sertima influences the academic debates in Harlem and study the African experiences, poetry, culture, music, history and rebellions, bring it into academic consideration and searching for Africa in world. This development led to the establishment of black studies, as highlighted earlier on in previous essay.

The Negritude movements in the hands of Amie Caesar, Leopold Senghor, Jean Paul Satre and of course the Pan African movement facilitates the journey of understanding African colonial conditions, and introduces the concept of Negritude in world humanism movement, the aim was to create a new world for Africans, a new soil for African confidence to grow. The issue of Negrituide was an a resurrective movement of African identities murdered by the Caucasians, and Africans themselves performs the funeral rites by emulating the western way of life. In doing so, Fanon (1962) provides a critical analysis from a psychological point of view, whereby the colonial conditions dehumanize Africans and make them the Wretched of the Earth, referred to as the people without soul hence to debunk such obnoxious structural system, Fanon suggest violent revolution and decolonize the way of thinking. The issue of the mind remains the contemplating issue in search of Africans in global publics, the discourse of black consciousness add a revolutionary perspective and develops the ideas on how to remake the African mind, due to the issue of rehumanizing the university, society and justice system towards the goal of liberating the African self. Reclaiming Africa is ontological and metaphysically defined, that make it different from what Hispanophone scholars proposes.

The differences motivated by complex metaphysical issues, whereby in Africa it was not just decolonize the mind, but political space and annihilate European existence in Africa. The life of pre-Berlin conference in Africa was molded by the cultural cosmologies as the reflection of the spiritual being in the context of social, political and economic issues. Kwasi Wiredu, Pauline Hauntondji, Theophile Obenga and John Mbiti propounds the existence of comprehensive institutions as a result of the existential phenomenon of African philosophy, which was denied its existence by European existence. Africans have their own way of defining God, as the highest being, the creator, the most gracious and the source of all materialistic life (Mbiti 1960). Africans have their own way of religious practices, death, rituals and issues of cosmic wisdom, that is even evidenced in Afro-Caribbean and Afro-Americans that still continue to carry out the practice of African religions, value and spirituality (Marimba 1994). This way of life, has defined a different form of epistemologies among people of African descent and Africans, and this furthers the need and realization of decolonizing the public intellectual spaces.

In European text, African spirituality viewed as mythical and mystical which lacks the systematic approach of religious system. Manganyi (1974) have this to say, the colonial encounters transform a cultural society and polarizing it into two, the urban and rural whereby in most cases rural populace remain immune to the western way of life and continue the practice of our very own sublime culture. The call for decolonizing the mind, championed by literature deacon Ngugi waThiongo, based on language, culture and memory, materializes and brings positive transformation in literary writings evidenced in the huge publication of stories in African indigenous language. The main theme or objective of this issue, was to challenge the existing linguistic hegemony and Europhonic aspect which act as the fertile grounds to continue the issue of coloniality.

> "Is African renaissance possible when we keepers of memory have to work outside our own linguistic memory? And within the prison house of European linguistic? If we think of the intelligentsia as generals in the intellectual army of Africa including foot soldiers, can we expect this army to conquer when it is worse when they level in their fate as captives" (Ngugi wa Thiong'o 2009;92)

The linguistic captivity of Africa, affect progress and the fruition of African Renaissance. African Renaissance as a term coined by the statement by Thabo Mbeki, pontificate the grand-rising of the continent from the periphery to an important global player. It is different from European Renaissance, since Europe by then were coming from dark ages, but in this issue the dark age of Africa is colonialism and slavery that burry the once golden ages in the continent. For it to be a possible phenomenon, wa Thiong'o (2009), Prah (2013 and 2018) suggests the linguistic decolonial movement, since language is the shelter of culture and memory, hence in doing so it is historical restorative process towards African renaissance. In recreating another world and propelling the engine of African Renaissance movement, it must be at the same decolonizes the mind, and not forgetting the aspect of language and memory. Fourth generation of African scholars must radicalize the discipline, not just as an academic movement but for social-political transformation.

> "Key argument is that the Africa is not only a social and political construction but also a victim of imposed identities and this reality has made African political trajectories to continue into a ceaseless direction of struggling to negotiate themselves above externally imposed singularities as part of resisting the reality of being 'fenced' in by particular identity markers which they have not chosen themselves" (Ndlovu Gatsheni 2013)

This means the decolonial movement is more than an academic struggle, but a continuous political struggle that seeks to resist from the yesteryears imposed identities that continue to impose serious sororities and polarization of the African people. This has to say, the Africans are still being located to the margins, and given labels and concepts, as objects for them (us) to exist, hence the radicalized movement is towards the completeness of the process and organized by academic researches, debates in Organization of Social Science Africa Research and other academic institutions, and push the curriculum reformist agenda. The Rhodes Must Fall and Fees Must Fall movements raises the generals and foot soldiers of decoloniality and epistemic rebellion, rebelling against the existing Euro-American forms of knowledge(s). Professor S J Ndhlovu-Gatsheni, Professor

Lwazi Lushaba and Professor Kwesi Kwa Prah and other African Eurocentric critics study the nomothetic and longitudinal aspect of Rhodes Must Fall and continue to call the existence of Africas humanity and place the continent on the map of world knowledge. African voices in the decolonial trajectories is in the standpoint of philosophical, reclaiming African linguistics, African images and reconnects the African intellectuals to the roots of African soil, and challenge the Eurocentric universal truth accreditation.

Is Decoloniality Patriarchal? A Critical Reflection of "Human Liberation"

Decoloniality is not subjective to human liberation, it's about liberating man and women from the complex of coloniality. Colonial spaces identifies the crudest propensity of women brutalization and marginalization structures on the global economy of knowledges and ontological existence of Eurocentric values. It is of no use to celebrate the eminent eruption of decolonial activism without even including the aspect of women emancipation.

Decoloniality is not patriarchal like other redemptive ideologies, it is based on the principles of universe as cosmos in its making whereby everyone in the society contributes to knowledge production. In this regard, it appetise the swift movement of the idea to decolonize post-colonial public spaces whereby the idea of post-colonial feminism in a deconstructionist paradigm gave rise to the need to decolonize academic society. The identification of colonial discourses inside the social mass movement regarding the public image of woman was an important stand point to broaden the scope of feminism and decolonization, whereby the idea of women emancipation was an outside context of the women of color (Ballerstein 2016, Harraway 2016, Lugones 1994). The colonial problems in subaltern societies was the issue of relegation of women to the bottom, and reduced to non-humans at the same time as black man. There are two historical situations to examine before we understand how women movement is part of 'decoloniality' and the movement towards epistemic justice (Grosfoguel 2013). The Fall Al Andalus in the Iberian Peninsula open the gates for the brutalization of women scholars. The event take place at the same time with the conquest of America by Christopher Columbus and the conquest of women in Europe. The conquest of woman manifest in crudest sense whereby women philosophers are insulted as witches, enemies of enlightenment, enemies of Christendom and burnt alive. These cruel behaviors constructed the patriarchal/Eurocentric canon of thoughts as world view and universal truth. History tell us that like Greek Philosophers, there were even great women scholars who played a pivotal role in the development of Enlightenment scholasticism and philosophy who are not included in the history of philosophers since patriarchal chauvinist Europeans erase that part of history. In studying objective history, it does not make any sense that the philosophy of history is male invention, and what constitutes society? What are the role of man and woman in the society?

Society constitutes man and women, which means both parties in harmony play a critical role in taming the environment, develops social relations, ethics and scientific invention. In history, searching women in pre-renaissance era is a mammoth task resulted in unsuccessful outcomes, where were there by then? Women begin to take part in history in the 18th century, that's how history is presented, but it's not even objective or true. In this regard, this historic account, after the fall of Al Andalus, is true and explains the real deal of the situation. It is one of the saddest moment in history. This important historical trajectory explains even the behavior of European In Caribbean colonies towards women (Anzaldua 1983, Dussel 1983). Apart from this crude historic moment, European avaricious tactics organized the colonial cartels to colonize Africa as to expand the market frontiers. In Pan Africana womanist perspective (Cresswel; sing 1994) women played a most decisive role in the making of African historiographies, there's no any race in the world who have the record of great female politicians, queens and war generals than Africa. For Samkange (1980), Tempels (154) and Kanagme (1964) the notion of Ubuntu (being human) cosmology premised on the idea of oneness and cosmos stracture of the society (I am because we are), and knowledge informed by cosmos interaction whereby everyone in the society played a critical role to the materialization of knowledges and social values. However the introduction of European capitalist/modernity in Africa shifted man and woman relations, from an equal basis to vertical relationship, women reduced as a property and relegated to the household chores.

It is of no surprise to argue that African antiquity were a paradisal society for women, whereby women played a critical role in the society as queens, leaders, war generals, spirit mediums and mothers. But all these glories have been jealously obliterated by the colonial gluttonous issues. The image of women in African past changed, it is even sad to read African Feminist writers omit this important issue in history of women liberation. The problem is the experts in gender studies have mastered the Eurocentric thoughts, whereby Europe is viewed as the center of knowledge and other global experiences remains in the periphery. It is prudent to dwell much on this historical material to argue and comprehend the broad concept of Decoloniality as humanist movement towards social justice. Social justice cannot be achieved if other groups are not included. Thomas Sankara purported that, Africa's liberation will be meaningless If it is not at the same time with women liberation. The situation in Africa and Europe is different, whereby man and women of color suffer serious dehumanization process from slave trade, colonialism, and today, its coloniality, hence every black social movement integrates everyone to fight the coloniality/patriarchal structures through different means.

> "I do not blame black man, what I'm saying is we have to take a new look at the ways in which we fight our joint oppression because If we don't we're going to blow each other up. We have to begin to redefine the terms of what women is, and what man is, how we relate to each other" (Baldwin).

James Baldwin put a discourse analysis of the liberation of movement informed by joint response of man and women against racist/patriarchal/coloniality institutions and erase the complex manifestation of coloniality of being.

The central dichotomy of modernity is the hierarchy between the human and non-human. Fighting against this modernity, decolonial movement integrates Afrocentric Womanism, Black Womanism and Pan Africana Womanism to define the image of African man and woman. In the course of decolonial history, Decoloniality is not sexist or patriarchal, it is socially universal and the oppressed, since coloniality of being and knowledge apply to everyone in third world countries, hence the theory is not gender specific but it is a humanist movement. Great scholars such as Gloria Anzaldua, Linda Tuhwai Smith, Reaewyn Connell, Clenoras Hudson, Marimba Ani, Maria Lugones, Francess Cresswelsing, Slyvia Wynter, Ama Mazama and Maria Tsolanova played an important role in the redefinition of feminism struggle, gender in decolonial epistemology and the issue of decolonality in post-anthropocentric episodes. Decoloniality is a contested dialectical philosophy aimed to restructure the world and it's ontological image to return to the originality as a place where humanism defines the purpose of every activity.

Conclusion

In conclusion, decolonial scholarship is not an independent discourse, from only to the one continent, but stretches as far across the high seas and oceans. The coloniaty oppressed groups realizes the need to rise, and challenge the existing norms and popular ideologies about the world. This essay points out that political and social transformation are the main aim of the revolutionary existence of epistemic reclamation project.

Chapter Five:
Social Transformation: An empirical survey of Midlands State University on decolonizing The university

Decolonizing the university embedded on social and political methodologies such as social activism through student unionism, questioning, theorizing, spirituality, erotics and the post-colonial theory of social change. Africa's post-colonial universities structures has been marred by the perpetuation of colonialism. Social transformation is the most important factor and ends in the process of decolonization, since it includes shift of thinking from the other to African self and, conceive the phenomenology aspect of experience explained in this chapter, to the dichotomy of 'coloniality and decoloniality'. Post-colonial trajectories witness various reforms in Africa as to meet post-colonial demands in newly independent states.

Chronicling decolonization of education in Africa commenced after independence by focusing on empirical survey, presenting research findings and atomizing the discourse of decolonizing the university in the post-colonial societies. This chapter's main objective is to give an analytical concept of the status of the university towards re-engagement with African being and thoughts. Through qualitative researches based on interviews, a practical manifestation of the theory is analyzed so as to embark on the morphological understanding of the phenomenology of decolonizing the university. This chapter is themed on the art and science of liberation, the politics of knowing from the rails of colonial slavery transcending to the case study of Midlands State University.

The Trajectory of Post-Colonial Universities Zimbabwe; Understanding the Epistemic Rebellion and Imagining A Decolonial Academic Space

The development of post-colonial university education in Africa prepare the way for liberating academic space from skirmish epistemic hegemony. Ndhlovu-Gatsheni (2016) devised a new concept called epistemic rebellion, whereby it really means the total reassertion of the lost ontologies and reclaiming African epistemology in imagining a decolonial institution. Shizha and Makuvaza (2013) narrate the technical development of state universities and end racial policy in entry requirements and administration. In comparative phenomenon, African universities in colonial era were primarily focused on alienating black communities to receive higher education whereby few blacks were privileged to be enrolled in higher education. This was the first injustice corrected, the collapse of political colonialism paved the way for social reformation, the right of education to occupy the epicenter of post-colonial sociology that increases black scholars among the communities.

Various universities were enacted to fulfill this obligation of massification of higher education. Transcending in Zimbabwe in the renaming of the then University of Zimbabwe, thus providing a ground breaking story in decolonizing the university, and invited huge enactment and coming of other state universities,. National University of Science and Technology, Midlands State University to mention a few. Churches and private organization played an impetus role to galvanize the alloy of decolonizing the university through establishing universities to meet the post-colonial demands of education. Voices from the margins were prioritized in post-colonial educational dynamics so as to promote critical masses and educated citizens to deconstruct various social imbalances that were crafted by colonial policies. Through the conceptualization of Professor Knowles's education theory, andragogy created an impressive imagination to the existence of new modern skills in industry through adult and open distance learning. Open distance learning centers were opened such as University of South Africa, Zimbabwe Open University, Zambia Open University, Nigeria Open University to nature skills on those who are already in the industry to promote innovation and development in post-colonial societies. The wave of democratization in post-colonial Africa created the existence of various civil society organizations to aid the process of democratization in Africa. Hwami and Kipoor (2006) justified student civil organization as the most important youth wing in democratizing academic space through activism.

Theorizing nationalism and decolonization, social activism strengthened movements of liberation across the continent, student activism in university education development acted as the major organization in decolonizing the university whereby it characterized the democratic movements and intellectual analysis, theories and questions. This is witnessed by various student movements and activism in South Africa continuing Black Consciousness Movement in post-apartheid era as to decolonize the curriculum that alienated

Africans from their culture. In the quest to promote higher education in post-colonial Zimbabwe, Midlands State University came into being in the year 2000 through Midlands State University Act of 2000. The university is located in Midlands's province of Zimbabwe.

The university came into being in the praxis to answer the need for higher education in Zimbabwe, since University of Zimbabwe and National University of Science and Technology were crowded and failed to deliver adequately the vision and responsibility of Ministry of Higher and Tertiary Education, Science and Technology Development. The university has various faculties namely, faculty of science and technology, faculty of natural resources and agriculture, faculty of medicine, faculty of commerce, faculty of education, faculty of social science, faculty of mining science, faculty of laws and faculty of arts. The university offer various degree programs, from bachelors, masters and PhD programs that make it a citadel of knowledge in Zimbabwe. The critical examination of the disciplines at the university proved the continuity of the coloniality of the university. As an institution it exists in post-colonial society, the theory of emptiness by Hannah Arendt justified no longer colonialism but not yet independence, whereby struggle for independence still continued to independence from the mental slavery. Eurocentric hegemony as dominant knowledge system, influenced knowledge making at the university since it inherited the colonial curriculum transferred to it by the University of Zimbabwe. Colonial curriculum was mainly focused on producing labour not thinkers that effected post-colonial trajectories in the university sociological schema. The labour production problematize genuine knowledge making characterized by theorizing, thinking and questioning, as the methodology in decolonizing the university in post-colonial societies. Independence is an unfinished business in the African societies due to the existence of invisible hand of imperialism and continual agony in all facets of life. However, various developments implements the objective of Africanizing the university as social transformation in post-colonial Zimbabwe.

The Dimension of Education 5.0 and the Future

Ministry of Higher and Tertiary Education, Science Development launches the new education policy based on narrowing the gap between academics and social realities, since the prevailing education was determined by the coloniality of epistemologies, produced half backed students who even failed to transform the theoretical knowledge into practical reality. The former tertiary education policy, was designed in 3.0 template, based on research, teaching and community services, however the current one is heritage based, and have five pillars namely, teaching, research, community service, innovation and industrialization. It seeks to modernize and industrialize Zimbabwe by having an Aligned and Productive Manpower from the universities. It is a decolonial strategy aimed to build better skills for national development through education with production.

National Crtical Skills Audit Summary Results in Zimbabwe

Sector	Availability	Surplus/Deficit
Engineering and Technology	6.43%	-93,5%

Natural Sciences	3.09%	-96.91%
Business and Commerce	121%	+21%
Agriculture	12%	-88%
Medical and Health Sciences	5%	-95%
Applied Arts and Humanities	82%	-18%
Average	38.25%	-61.75%

Source, *Ministry of Higher and Tertiary Education*

This table, shows the skills deficit in Zimbabwe, there's still a huge gap in natural sciences and engineering. Education 5.0 aims to reduce -67.75% skills deficit in Zimbabwe, through a heritage based education system and introduces the pillars of innovation and industrialisation. In doing so, the issue of innovation hubs is in due course to all state universities and facilitates the goal towards filing the gap of skills deficit in Zimbabwe. To achieve this, programme infrastructure is the key drivers whereby curriculum aligned to demanding skills in the society to all programmes and disciplines, the second one is promotion of infrastructure system, such as innovation hub to refine the ideas for industrial development, and lastly financing infrastructure to fund the development of ideas. This project is a decolonial project aimed to answer the national question of development and the idea of Zimbabwe. This policy is a welcome move towards epistemic rebellion, and have prospective span of recreating African epistemologies and re-center the analysis of science and values of the continent.

Research Philosophy and Methodology.

Research philosophy basis research foundation or framework of question formulation, data presentation and analysis, as theories of epistemology premised on positivism that is experimentation and, conclusions that usher in new knowledge and interpretivists based on normative analysis (anti-positivism). The purpose of this study is understood on the concept of ontology based on realist approach and normative concepts that help the researcher to understand the existence of metaphysics (natural world) and the creation of norms and values encompassed by the integration of norms and values in educational, academic axioms and institutions. It is believed that, human nature understood the issue of environmental determinism whereby the environment influenced human behaviour or human behaviour influenced the environment, this concept of research philosophy helps in the study to produce a comprehensive phenomenon and philosophical sagacity on epistemic development of the logic of decolonizing the university. Approaches to Social Science and Research integrated to come up with an accurate thesis, in question construction, events analysis (ideographic and nomothetic strands of debate). Interviews, observations and surveys were conducted to produce an empirical framework of this study.

Theorizing the Phenomenology of Decolonizing the University at MSU.

1. Narrating African Anthropology

Research is the most important approach employed by post-colonial universities to embrace epistemic freedom, however Professor Linda Tuhwai Smith questioned the credibility of research in constructing histories of the indigenous people, since this research premised on world views that distorts images and perceptions of Truth. Smith (2010) decolonizing research methodologies influences this section, whereby research on African Anthropology at MSU is weighed towards an epistemic rebellion theory. MSU ventures in knowledge making and contribute immensely to the rewriting of the African past as a research institution in post-colonial Zimbabwe. Midlands State University as a research institution shapes and promotes social and cultural research through qualitative and quantitative methodology. Social and cultural research promotes the narratives of African anthropology on the themes of culture, race, origins, philosophy, post-colonial society and post-modern projection. Social Science and Humanities embrace more on social and cultural researches, since it is people's organization oriented. Disciplines such as Political Science, Public Management, Geography, Social Ecology, Music and Musicology, Media, Anthropology, Sociology engages in the repositioning of disciplines to be African oriented. In an Interview with Patricia Masiyakurima on Afrocentric point of view, she posits:

> "Research is acknowledged as the best method in decolonizing the university, since it caters for rewriting

African history and demystifies the masterpiece publication that erase Africans' place in the history of civilization".

However, what informs that research? And whose world view? An Afrocentric theory should be embraced to create Afro-centered space in analyzing African issues as to rewrite the distorted African past. This clearly explains the objective of decolonizing the university, as an art to dismantle the dominant thinking of Africa as a continent without historical conscience. Hence Midlands State University plays a pivotal role to galvanize the alloys of phenomenology of decolonizing the university through engaging in refocusing the shift of Eurocentric thinking in African universities. Research areas such as Politics, governance, society, labour and other social studies engages in intellectual programs that enables researchers to enhance the genesis of African epistemology and decolonial thoughts.

Faculty of Arts, disciplines such as History, International Studies, African Languages and Culture, English and Communication, Film and Theatre Arts, Theology and Archaeology promotes a distinct and unique research on culture and society. Normativism, as research philosophy employed by hermeneutic conception of history, culture and society, act as the methodology in creating new epistemic-ontologies through developing historical and cultural theories. Issues such as heritage, gender, development, religion, language and visual arts must be embraced into the curriculum and be refined through research. Interviewing Professor Percslage Chigora a Political Scientist at Midlands State University, stated that,

> "University researchers are the agency of knowledge making and decolonial thought in decolonizing text books,

they promote the interaction and restoration of the lost ontologies"

In this regard cultural facets in Africa researched partly pre-colonial histories using historiographical research methods like archaeology, oral tradition and written records. Remember the dismembered fashioned research ethics used to criticize the dominant philosophy of African mind that was presented by Hegel on primitive mentality, as the absurdity of African being in debates and academic society.

A glance at Professor Peter Garlake research on pre-colonial Great Zimbabwe society, culminating in the debates about who constructed Great Zimbabwe, by using archaeological research and analysis. In this regard, Film and Theatre, History, International Studies and African languages and Culture play a pivotal role in the reconstruction and rewriting of African history and culture through filming cultural epic films and researches. "People who don't know their history are like a tree without roots" Marcus Garvey said. Rethinking Marcus Mosiah Garvey, it is quite a sorry case to the people who lost the traits of their history due to catastrophic amnesia caused by colonial subjugation. Institutions taught African European history rather than African History, hence social and cultural researches promote the reconstruction and rewriting of history and debunk Eurocentric historical monologue. In most cases, a number of generations were affected by African European History, contributed to the existence of coloniality of being, whereby the ontological density of global Manichean misanthropy of zones (being and non-beings) won ballots in global sociology (Maldonado-Torres; 2016). In this regard, research influence social and cultural practices of academia and society.

It is the role of institutional researchers from undergraduate to post-graduate studies to research on lost pride, heritage and culture to influence on transmodernity social anthropology and reclaim African epistemology.

> "Eurocentric groups emerges for defending specific interest, hence massive researches should be accounted to defend the principle of humanity" (Interview with Dr Godfrey Chikowore; Humanistic perspective"

In this regard, historical traits of Eurocentric ideology premised on defending and dissolving other centric viewpoints in world view that affect the theory of humanism in global society. University research liberate the global epistemic structure through questioning and theorizing the concept and solipsistic belief. Historical research in academic concept act as the methodology in decolonizing education. A number of text in colonial era influence social system, such as Das Capitol (Marxism on Social Democracy) and other decolonial books influence the structure of the society hence social and cultural researches are on the fore front of university curriculum pages to reconstruct the lost ontologies.

The thrust of archaeological research is to reconstruct the lost ontologies and history of pre-colonial societies. Historical projects funded by the Universities and research institutes of Archaeology, Heritage and Museum Studies research on pre-colonial societies through epistemological reconstructions in book reviews and archaeological visits in pre-colonial sites. Trips on heritage sites and research in archaeological sites such as Sphinx, Pyramids and Great Zimbabwe Ruins should be done to recollect the past historiographies and document it, and promote the achievement of objective of decolonizing university project. In this regard the discourse of archaeological researches play a part in epistemic freedom through reconnecting with the past, present and future in historiographical narrative and ontological reclamation in documents and learning. The role of ethnomusicology as academic discipline reconnects the present theatrical studies with the past through understanding social gathering norms and the purpose of Music. Ethnomusicology recollects the meaning choreographies such as Mhande, Mbende and Muchongoyo in the understanding of past-histories through visual art performing and researches. The discourse of decoloniality of education embraced post-colonial universities in the bid to create a true sense of post-colonial education that is in line with epistemic freedom and recollection of the past histories.

2. Economics and Political Research

National policy research as the major aspect aim to provide solutions on political economic problems, as a think tank and research institution it provide a basic approach of the relationship between education and development. Universities play a pivotal role in researching on policy abrogation and policy evaluation. For instance the vision of MSU in research is to provide a multidisciplinary approach to national policies such as ZIMASSET (Zimbabwe Agenda for Sustainable Social Economic Transformation), Gender National Policy (GNP), Look East Policy and other policies so as to offer recommendations on results based management evaluation process. Universities as research institutes galvanize the alloys of decolonizing education through research, based on focus group discussion, and the role of academics in shaping national and foreign politics is to award educational institutional research. In post-colonial reconstruction, academic research embrace Pan African thoughts in research that creates a strong bond to research and decolonizing education.

Political researches, based on post-colonial political architect are research interest of students and lecturers on the aspect of nationalism, democracy and post-colonial political violence. In this regard, research findings corroborate the research as the methodology of decolonizing education in innovation in international and political affairs.

International research and thesis should be designed to create a theoretical framework on contemporary issues that affect Africa. The commitment of the university towards international relations from undergraduate to post-graduate research is to engage in African personality theory, produce African theories for African problems. Professor Chigora commented:

> "International relations and political science researches are a genuine tool in developing the redemptive strategies of decolonizing political concepts, publications and writing since a number of texts in library serves are in the interest of the western world to programme the Eurocentric mentality to the university students".

This realistic observation, explores the effort of the university in promoting the phenomenology of decolonizing the university by questioning European publications and international relations theories of governance and politics.

3. Embracing Scientific Researches. Positivist Epistemology and Science Development

Research aims to promote global standards in science development and technology research. Scientific knowledge that is grounded on positivist approach based on experimentation of the object (Metaphysics). In transmodernity, global epistemologies based on scientific and technical development is influenced by industrial revolutions.

Hard sciences emerges as disciplines to understand the logic behind nature and physical existence in global phenomenology. Geometric research, chemical technology, bio-technology, Agric-technology, medicine, computer technology, digital technology and other scientific research technology promoted at the university are done to initiate scientific researches for national development.

The issue of scientific research inaugurate the new era in decolonial thought, since scientific researchers are different to Social Sciences and Humanities, based on global and unique epistemologies. In Social sciences and Humanities traditional thoughts are embraced in scientific research. Research engagement plays a pivotal role in decolonizing education. Internet Communication Technology (ICT) contributed to the establishment of technological programs such as Computer Science, Telecommunication and Information Technology in African Universities.

In the bid to promote scientific and technological researches, those programs enhanced higher learning of technology to decolonize education by promoting innovations among students, lecturers and university research. Technology promotes a unique system in the field of education and influences society, it promotes scientific developments in society.

The matrix of decolonial thought embraced by refocusing on sciences for national development, the demand of the modern ages in agriculture and biotechnology invent education with production in the national development discourses. Innovation and researches in the field of botany, crop science, animal science, parasitology, medical laboratories, livestock management and other scientific research prepare the way for decolonizing the university. Modern industry and global structure are scientific epistemologies based on facts and it is unique and different to Social Science and Humanities. The discourse of decoloniality of education encapsulated in scientific research at the universities promote technological and natural scientific research.

4. Industrial Exposure and Entrepreneurial Studies

Industrialism introduced in the form of industrial attachment as a way to build experience, harmonizes theory and practical in the realm of studies. The so called theoretical faculties are repositioned to focus on industrial development and practical orientation. Dr Richard Muranda, Lecturer in the Department of Music and Musicology states that:

> "Industrial attachment proved to be the solution in consolidating decolonization of the university, through engaging in industrial exposure that promotes creativity"

A number of African universities adopt the concept of work related learning to erode the parallel existence of education and development. Midlands State University adopts the strategy to galvanize the alloys of decolonizing the university, as to refurbish the connection between industry and education.

> "...since Faculties of Arts and Social Sciences termed theoretical faculties in colonial times and create the concept of job seeking mentality, Midlands State University introduced Entrepreneurship course to create open mindedness, innovation and demystifying the aspect of theoretical faculties" (Interview with D Nkala Lecturer on the department of Entrepreneurship Studies at MSU)

Entrepreneurial studies emerge as a discipline to equip the minds of the student with business minds, creativity and innovativeness as a way to adjust the role of education in contribution to the national fiscal gains. Broadening the aspect of decolonizing the university, the scope of African epistemology is modernized to the scope of practicality and pragmatic contribution to the development of the nation.

Imagining the future of Decoloniality at MSU

Attempts to implement Africanization of the university have been battled down by numerous challenges, ranging from Anti-decolonial resistance and continuity of coloniality of being, whereby the so called middleman in the making of the other still hold the administrative power of the institution hence decolonizing the university remain an uneasy task. Social science and humanities disciplines exert pressure to exhume Africanity in academic affairs but western epistemology is still on the rail. Western epistemology and methodology affect the process of decolonization of education in African universities. The methods for epistemic freedom such a researches, has been countered by Eurocentric thought, declared as the most important academic thoughts by the victim administrators and lecturers. To examine, departments of psychology, political science and philosophy, there's still a great residue of coloniality that affect the process of curriculum development designed to decolonize the disciplines, whereby major theorist from these named disciplines are from the West, and their knowledge structure is centered on the Euro-American canon of thoughts.

> According to Professor P Chigora, "The knowledge system should be cosmos (which means everyone is included, children, woman and disabled) as to promote creativity and decolonizing the knowledge, however the journey is too tense since post-colonial professors educated from western universities carry the cargoes of western epistemologies that was offloaded to the shores of African universities"

In this regard, the western knowledge systems lacks the cosmic (it is patriarchal in nature) feature that prepare the silent obituary of other knowledge systems to prevail in the society, it lacks subversity and pluriverse features. Western epistemology finds a way to continue in reformed curriculum to create an obstacle to the project of decolonizing education at MSU. This aspect creates a miscarriage of decolonial project. The miscomprehension and misconception of differences of epistemology in academic discourse create a further delay of the process, since focus group discussion create a long standing debate over the aspect of how epistemology should be different. According to observations, MSU learning system is influenced by western universities approach, which creates mental slavery. Political entourages affect the concept of decolonizing the university since it influences publication and the interest in epistemology. Issues of political censorship in Zimbabwe affect knowledge generation whereby interest groups, teaching methods are captured with politics that produce a narrow and linear mindset on world view. MSU produce graduates who are affected by 'politicization' of knowledge system, whereby certain publication of African socialism fear to criticize the government and publish in political interest of the politician. Student unions such as Zimbabwe Congress of Student Union (ZICOSU) and Zimbabwe National Student Union (ZINASU) affects knowledge generation by creating linear mentality either on conservative and political activism. The Universities becomes a beacon of political playground demystifying the truth rather than to focus on searching and researching the truth. Issues of high politics in Zimbabwe creates an obituary to knowledge system, the influence of politics in research is based on partisan and linear perspective. Weaponization of revolution in politics affects the knowledge banks of publishing true research papers on the subjects and concepts.

The decolonial project problematized by politicization of knowledge system remain a superstition at the university. As highlighted by Mahomva (2014), the relationship between Pan Africanism and decolonial project is based on cultural and intellectual movement, however the intellectual movement at Midlands State

University is affected by politicization of knowledge(s). MSU is a research think tank, and as a research institutions it contributed immensely to national development through policy research; but unfortunately issues of high politics transforms the aspect of melodramic nightmares. It is now a myth, and the meaning of the university in Zimbabwe community has failed to make sense, it has only becomes a passport of status creation. The elites produced by the universities, however are alienated to the African culture that continues the procreation of the ontology of the other in global economy of knowledge.

The debate about language revolves in the objective of whether to mobilize linguistic nationalism or not, since the language system succeed in promoting the other. On this aspect of language, the use of English language is not to be denied, but generally the adoration of indigenous language at MSU is in bad state. At Midlands State University the epistemic freedom struggle is affected by linguistic coloniality, since English language is used as teaching and learning language. In an Interview with Professor Chigora and Professor Charles Tembo they highlight the concept of naiveté and dishonest in teaching that serves western interests.

> "Education system to embrace decolonizing education at the university is a difficult task since western cultures incorporated in learning and teaching at the university, the aspect of English language and the western language problematize the objective of decolonizing the university" (Interview; Ngonidzashe Machingauta)

This radical view makes sense in discourse of Africanity and the struggle to create African being, however in real perspective, since this research is focusing on practicality of the study other views emerge.

> "English Language open up capabilities for global interaction" (Interview with Dr Godfrey Chikowore).

English language has won fame in global relative theory as it is used for re-engaging in multicultural world, and connecting different races together through speaking one language. From the relative theory, a Multicultural Afrocentric appreciation brings in the new thought on the debate of language at Midlands State University.

> "There's the existence of 'Englishes' in Africa, not English. Multiplicity of version of Englishes" (Interview with Professor Charles Tembo).

In this regard it should be used as a teaching language, however developing our own language and vocabulary diction, so as to embrace the decolonial project in post-colonial societies.

Conclusion

As a far gone conclusion, research shows the academic development of the institution and rethinks African agency in remaking African academic institutions. Issues of reach and curriculum development designed is the objective of decolonizing the university. However some of the challenges are such as the question of language, epistemology and politics. The pertinent problem of epistemological institutions and coloniality in the mind affect the fruition of academic excellence in Sub-Saharan Africa. The concept of diasporic and Afro-pessimism and developmental conundrum owed much from Afro-western historicity and present ties. To corroborate on this issue, the prerogative evidence of coloniality of education continues to produce alienated educated masses with western epistemology. In recommendatory note, indigenous language, curriculum should reforms in integrating anthropology courses across all faculties to create avenues of decolonizing the university.

Chapter Six:
Redefine the Image of African being from the 'other'

What's wrong with our image? Why do we need to redefine the African Being? These logical questions creates the epistemological domain of this essay, whereby previously it is explained that sub-humanity, inferiority and the *Wretched of the Earth* define Negro/Orient/Subaltern conditions, as non-thinking objects and subjects to global capitalistic structures. For decolonizing the university, the image of these societies need to be redefined basing on cultural aesthetic and historical legacy. Theorizing decolonization of the university in the post-colonial era owes practical magnum that creates critical activism as the reincarnation of anti-apartheid and anti-colonial movement in Sub-Saharan Africa. Developmental paradoxes has been complicated as Africa face developmental conundrum, generated by coloniality of being and power through mental slavery and epistemicide channeled through universalization of Eurocentric canon of thoughts in all academic disciplines. In (Re)thinking decolonizing the university and epistemic freedom, the pleasure of epistemic freedom may be seen through the expanse of creativity of Africanity ontologies, reconstruction of the image and aesthetic of the African being from the "other" through revolutionary university, truth and opinion about the world view and the meaning of the society. What is an African being? African being is the art and expressions of Africanity (identities) in social and political matters, and defines the phenomenology of Africaness through the consciousness of being-in-itself (soul and spirit of Africa) and being-for-itself (the purpose in the African cosmology). From the previous chapter, it is explained that slavery, colonialism and global coloniality projects affects the image of African being, characterize it with barbarism, primitivity and lack of skills, however decolonizing the university drills new image in the world view whereby the story of Africa before colonialism need to be publicized to decolonizing being, and knowledge. Post-colonial universities engage in massive reforms to fulfill developmental objectives of newly independent states, an attempt to decolonize the university has been propagated in the pendulum of educational reforms and policies. Reforming racist policies, engage in anthropological and scientific researches to pragmatise the so called theoretical faculties that aid the process of decolonizing the university. However the situation remains tense, the struggle for Uhuru continues, since those attempts have been wrestled down by numerous challenges. Post-colonial trajectories face rift and huge gulf on education and development, that paralyze developmental confidence in Africa. This section is mandated to develop and redefine African being and theorize the decolonizing the university in intellectual perspective.

Re-making African Being, Anthropological Paradigm

It's now a re-making, with the suffix 're' which means African being existed before, that help us to construct the great histories of Egypt,

Mali, Songhay, Sudan and Munhumutapa, hence there's need to remake, re-define African being in global social spaces. Revisiting the European being, it is constructed from the strong foundation of cultures and values that make it strong, and forever remains strong which promotes creativity in Europe. To transcend this issue in African discourse, the creation of African being should be constructed at the same time with strong cultural foundation and values of the society.

Reflecting the systematic expression of African being in the art and science of living is defined in threefold (1) a system, (2) being and (3) idea. History is the present created by ideas, hence the discourse of "idea" in human society is the most important philosophy to understand and define the society. African being as an idea, exist as an intellectual and social theory aimed to create a proper image of African being idea in both academic world and social world. The idea of an African being put forward in this essay is extension of black consciousness theory and creates social place for true African being in the world. The world is divided in two camps, in economic perspective there's the developed and developing nations (Quinjano 2000). In Politics and sociology there's global citizens and the subject. According to Mandani (1998), colonial legacy divides the society in two systematic groups based on race, citizens and the subject. Global citizens are the west since the west is the center of modern civilization and modernity, hence Caucasians are defined as superior race.

The prognosis of dialectics condition of the world in sociology problematize the theory of humanity since the structure of human and sub-humans structures are nourished by capitalist/patriarchal structure. From post-structural point of view, colonized states are still called subjects because there are inferior and subjected to western values and philosophies of life. Africans are subjects because there are alienated from their culture. African being as an idea is aimed to recreate the status of citizenry that enhances the orientation of black race as global competitors in global affairs. Marcus Mosiah Garvey once said, "Black skin is not a badge of shame, but a symbol of superiority". The idea of African being is designed in the objective of exhuming the posterity of black superiority in global society. As a system and being, it is composed on (re)programming African intellectual scholarship in the universities, through adopting Afrocentric paradigm in teaching and learning. This conception raise the soul of African folk to redefine themselves as true Africans in the world of their own, not a world designed by the west to maintain hegemonic penchant. Theoretical discourses of African being as a system, seen in pragmatic expression of African intellectual devotees such as Cheikh Anta Diop, Molefe Kete Asante, Marimba Ani, to mention a few engages in rewriting African history and reinventing theories such as Pan African intellectual thoughts, 'Yurugu' cultural analysis and Afrocentric theory of Remember African Agency. Those erudite act as agents in African being making process. Eurocentric thoughts forced to go back and sail within western boarders resulted in scholarship that debunks western thoughts. The concept of black consciousness, as a system, influences contemporary social and intellectual activism in decolonizing the university. Manganyi (1961) and Wynter (2010), said blackness in the world defined in western aesthetic is inferiority, barbaric and primitive, and is supported by the Hegelian historical view. However, on psychological being Manganyi (1974) and Wynter (2010) argue that, blackness as the original being affected by a series of events such as slavery, colonialism and neo-colonialism is reduced to dames. African being as an ideology, a system and a person focus on African agency in global thoughts, arguments and theorizing of African space in global economy of knowledge.

The metaphysical connection of Africa as landmass and the people that live there, creates a relationship between identity and being, hence African being. There's strong connection between the reconstruction of African being and anthropological paradigms, since anthropogenic activities play a pivotal role in the making of being and society. I will revisit anthropological paradigm, a progressive thought in (re)making the African being in global society. Anthropological paradigms excavate the skeletal remnants of African being, to add flesh and soul in philosophical society. Musical anthropology is the cardinal principle and parallel dimension in reconstructing African being, to decolonize disciplines and re-writing historical narratives. Re-writing African historiography poses a holy scripture and daily bread to fed the African soul in African being, it (re)programs the African ontologies to fabricate the African being. Since the world polarised in two camps, western modernity and global south primitive, that myth problematizes the existence of strong two beings. Since previous chapter explained the lack of originality of "other" being, either western view or African view, hence the programming of new thoughts through expanse anthropology play a pivotal role in (re)making African being. Ethno-music and choreographies of theatrical performance exhibits the past history of great African Queens and Kings as well as spiritual cosmology. Singing the past in the prism of Afrocentric theory, remember the dismembered (Asante, 2007). Molefe Kete Asante theorizes Afrocentric theory as to rebuild African Agency in African stories, hence an ethno-musicological concepts act as the oral historiography methodology in reconstructing African anthropology.

African history and narrative accounts have been distorted, however the traditional musical performances tells us the full detail of the stories, and remakes the African being. The significance of traditional instrumentation has no doubt in feeding the spiritual existence of African soul. The instrumentation, Mbira, Marimba, Hosho, Ngoma and magagada creates a unique and deep cultural poly-rhythm which reconnects modern day with the past, injects the compilation of musical archives and researches. Agawu (2010), a leading scholar in African musicology credited for his argument in replaying African rhythm as anthropological activities to conserve the cultural remnants, so as to introduce the originality of African being in dehumanized societies. Remember the dismembered sloganize the decolonization movement. The performance contain deep cultural language and customs that engage in the creation of past imagination, and help anthropologist to narrate about the past, poetry and linguistic diction. The posterity of African musicology act as the great source of rewriting African history and decolonizing the university. Tracing Shona anthropology through ethno-musicology anthropological research, cultural music such as Chaminuka Ndimambo performed by Lenos Wengara, *Mhondoro dzinomwa kunasave* and *Mudzimu Dzoka* exhibits the past social organization of the Shona people in prehistoric era. Applying Afrocentric methodology in social science research philosophy, musical anthropology produce a longitudinal thought in reconstructing African historiographies as it is evidenced by various Shona, Ndebele, Zulu and Kikuyu cultural philosophy. The artifacts, programs a memory of African art and aesthetic, which engage in massive procreating of African being in decolonized institutions.

Humanizing the University in (re)making African Being.

Reengaging in Africanity polishes the cultural aesthetic in decolonizing the university. Humanizing the university is referred to the re-connection of the education system and the glory of cultures. It has been discovered that current education curriculums are designed to alienate African cultures that consolidate epistemic violence. Ngugi Wa Thiongo argued that culture is a symbol of existence, hence without culture there's no existence, one asks the question that "Does Africa Exist?". This question raise the concern over African existentialism and assign scholars to research on the residue of African culture and redefine Africanity, that proved futile due to cultural imperialism that affected modern generation. Cultures defines existence of certain societies, to define Europeans resulted from culture, in order to define someone as Indian it's not skin complexion but culture. In African perspectives, the existence is shown by blackness or cartographic existence, the cultural inexistence or imperialism burry the soul of existence in Africa. Hence it is the mandate of citadels of knowledge to reclaim African existence and to humanize the educational dialectic through cultural re-orientation programs. In humanizing the university, African cultural ontologies re-oriented in learning system and environment as to reclaim true African identity and recreate Africa. Emperor Haile Selassie once said "African awaits its creators", means it is yet to be created, creators are yet to come. Decolonizing the university creates a pervasive way of creating Africa in post-Modernities.

Humanizing the art and theory of education premised on Afrocentric paradigm in the objective to re-connect Africa to the past glory. To thaw the icebergs of colonialism of African agency to cease to exist in academic affairs by reclaiming identities. African ethics clothed by various ethical beliefs, justified by Henry Odera Oruka (Oruka 1990) as a means to humanize the university, create universities as cultural centers of the continent. Cultural carnivals, poetry, theatre and music to be developed by the responsible departments to impart the knowledge and glory of Africa. Reclaiming African humanity and identities theatricalized by carnivals as cultural exhibition transform African being from other self to African self. Tracing Uhuru, humanizing the university provides a theoretical framework for the pragmatic expression for decolonizing the university in Africa and reconstructing African being.

The Image of A Decolonial 'Uni-versity', A Polycentric Paradigm

There is need of re-making of the university, based on decolonizing the university and establishing knowledge making institutions that universalize social epistemic variation and polycentricism. According to Lushaba (2017), the template of knowledge should be written anew, based on pluriversalism so as to create the 'university' in post-humanistic society. Against the background of Eurocentric epistemologies, dominated by countries that problematize the conceptual application and the meaning of 'university' as training institutions, hence a multicultural ideologies has to be employed. Multi-cultural heritage provides a state interconnectedness bonafide circumstance, which bury the solipsistic and cultural arrogant skirmishes in global era. To swiftly decolonize the university it is of best practice to open the gates of various thoughts from races and different cultural groups. Accept Asia centric, Eurocentric and Latino centric perspective in global knowledge system at the same time embrace more on Afrocentric template of knowledge. Post-humanism society, defined as the society refine itself to bring different races together and acknowledging each other as equal global players. In reconstructing African being, theorizing a multicultural society engages in the genuine production of global epistemologies, fashioned in the subverse of the universe.

> "Pluriverse is not a cultural relativism, but entanglement of several cosmologies connected today in a power different. That power deferential is the logic of coloniality covered by rhetorical narrative of modernity. Modernity is a fiction that carries in it the seed of western pretense to university …If a pluriverse is not a world of independent units (cultural relativism) but a world entangled through and by the colonial matrix of power, then, a way of thinking and understanding that dwells in the entanglement in the borders, is needed. So the point is not so to "study" borders that's very fashionable today, while at the same time "dwelling" in a territorial epistemology (which) would imply that you accept a pluriverse (as) some place out there that you accept, a pluriverse some place out there that you "observe" from some place outside the pluriverse "(Mignolo; 2013).

Walter Mignolo as the creature of school of dependency, focus on designing a decolonial institution that clearly produce students and lecturers who are capable to see the world in multiple lens and embrace multicultural world view to build a sophisticated truth about the universe. Remaking African being and decolonizing the university should be at the same time at re-making the university so as to produce a quality being in global society. If it is not done so, the truth will always be annihilated and recreates another form of being that has similar characteristics with Eurocentric being. Nelson Mandela states that, education is the most powerful weapon which you can use to change the world, hence a decolonized education system improves and engages in truthful view of the society, reorients it to the sociology of humanism and ideal society. That education should be pluriverse to change the world thinking and creates the African being. The phenomenology of decolonizing the university, center itself on being comprised of object and subject; hence the conception of re-making the university a panacea to create a new world of thoughts that are meaningful and decentering the alienation of Africans and global South from their cultures in learning system.

The world is moving towards one society, hence epistemologies should be in the rails of different cosmological schema around the globe to equip scholars on comprehending other society's values and beliefs as part of unique ethnic groups. The misunderstanding of the Arab world and terrorism misplaced, since Huntington (1996) put forward the theory of clash of civilizations. Western perspective of the society and Arabic perspective of the society clashes and plunge the world into the plague of anarchy and so called terrorism. This issue in academic affairs, partly African societies should be addressed to produce quality truth from opinions and philosophical reflections of the society. For one to understand the Arabic, or Islamic society you need to be well versed with Islamic philosophy of the society. In creating African being multiculturalism is to be integrated to meet the demands of the new global ecologies. The theory of Africa as Dark Continent is another epitome of mono-cultural misconception since European theologians failed to see the sense of African religion and civilization since there were well versed with Eurocentric knowledge that put only Europe and the West at the center of arts, civilization and philosophy of humanity. In remaking the African being, Afrocentric theory display the need to venture in the ecology of multiculturalism to build unique epistemologies and understanding of other cultures. Asante (2007), rethinks and theorizes Afrocentric theory as an ethno-valorized thought that reject other centric views like Eurocentric, its mandates is to survive in multicultural heritage. *Road to Babel* has been cleared, hence it is of paramount importance to engage in multicultural epistemology to understand Asian philosophy, European philosophy and Latin philosophy in the center of knowledge. To understand the sociogenic activities of other ethnic and racial groups without the conception methods applied by Eurocentric scholars. Integrating the multicultural approach to create a new thinking and theorize it in the meaning of the social world and enhance the creation of African being in post-colonial university.

Conclusion; Mapping the Contours of Decolonial Alternatives

Mapping the contours of decolonial alternatives and imagining the decolonial institution is still difficult, since various scholars proposes different theories that are parallel to each other, but sometimes are in harmony, yet there's no balance. This collection of essay are not aimed at providing a solid image or a decolonized institution, but to lay out some principles that fuel the process of epistemic freedom movement. Embedded on rewriting African histories, decolonizing being and influence is the departure from mono-centric world view but polycentric view. In decolonizing the university, venture in practical expression of the theory, the issues of humanizing the university, venture in anthropological paradigms and multicultural appreciation among others. Engaging in social activism and intellectual movement in decolonizing the mind, the university scholars should think of multicultural appreciation, anthropological paradigm of African society and cultural manifestation as the African Agency in Social Change. Creating the African being, a sensible, flexible, root connection and speaking the metaphysics of Africa as a panacea to circumvent the crisis of Africanity conundrum in African scholarship.

Decolonizing the university aims to create the new being, able to lead the African society into prosperity due to native and African epistemology possessiveness. As a concluding chapter of this enlightening collection of essays, the being is composed of object and subject which defines the phenomenological concept. So as to establish African being, this chapter is a theoretical development of understanding the concept, decolonizing the university is the most important methodology. Epistemic Freedom should be a national agenda since it focuses on the politics of freedom of the mind and body, as well as embrace the cordial relationship between education and development. One might wonder why public services fail to produce quality output; it's because they were miseducated from those westernized universities that we claim as our own national product. In this regard, a collective consciousness is needed to circumvent current tragedies in the continent.

However, the university, scholars and Afrocentric trained scholars need to rethink the concept, model it to the world class environment, and provide a meaning of what we call a decolonized institution. In this monography, decolonizing the university definition is centered not on Africanizing, but developing a template of knowledge that tolerate other centric views and denounces epistemic hegemony and universalization of Western centered truth. The curriculum system that encompass African knowledge(s) at the centre , and also include other knowledge(s) in Post-Cartesian episode. I believe, the education system we are in right now is not our own, we need to re-engage in the meaning of education that is our own as Africans. Before doing so, ecology should be sanitized to create a conducive environment for the business of university to produce quality products (students).

Bibliography

Alhassan, A. M. (2012) *Factors Affecting adult learning and their persistence. A Theoretical Approach.* European Journal of Business and Social Science, Vol 1(6) pp150-168

Akbar, N. (1984) *Chain and Images of Psychological Slavery*, London; New Mind Productions.

Anzaldua, G. (1987) Borderlands/La Frontera; New Mestiza; Aunt Lute Books

Asante, M. K. (1991) *"The Afrocentricity Idea in Education"*, Journal of Negro Education.

_____(2000) *the Egyptian Philosophers; Ancient African Voices Imhotep to Akhenaten;* Illinois; African American Images.

_____ (2006) *Cheikh Anta Diop; an Intellectual Portrait;* Los Angeles; University of Sankore Press.

_____(2003*) Afrocentricity; the Theory of Social Change*, Illinois; African American Images

_____(2007) *an Afrocentric Manifesto.* Cambridge; Polity Press

_____(2016) *Decolonizing the University in Africa; An Approach to Transformation* in M.K. Asante and Ledbetter, C. (2016*) Contemporary Critical Thought in Africology and Africana Studies,* London; Rowman and Littlefield Publishers

Bessis, S. (2003) *Western Supremacy. The Triumph of An Idea.* London and New York; Zed Books,

Brahl, L. (1923) *Primitive Mentality; Anthropology.* London; Allen and Unwin

Carnoy, M and Sammoff, J. (1991) *Education and Social Transition in Third World*. Princeton, NJ: Princeton University Press.

Chawame, M. (2016) *the Development of Afrocentricity*; A Historical Survey

Chitanana, L and Museva, L. (2012) *Adult education Students Perceptions of E-learning; a case study of Midlands State University*.

Chukwokolo, (2009) *Afrocentrism or Eurocentrism. The Dilemma of African Development*. New Journal of African Studies

Chomsky, N. (2000) *New Horizons in the Study of Language and Mind*, Cambridge; Cambridge University Press

Derrida, J. (1972) *Margins of Philosophy*. Chicago: Chicago University Press

Dibash, H. (2015) *Can Non-Europeans Think?* Zed Books

Diop, A. C. (1974) *the Origins of Civilization, Myth or Reality*. Chicago; Chicago University Press

_____. (1981) *Civilization or Barbarism; An Authentic Anthropology*. Chicago; Chicago University Press

_____. (1997) *the Peopling of Ancient Egypt and Deciphering of the Meroitic Script*, Chicago; Chicago University Press

_____. (1988) *Precolonial Black Africa;* Paris; Presence Africaine.

Dussel, E. (2003) Philosophy of Liberation, Wipf and Stock Pub

Dwain, A. P. (2007) *an analysis of Afrocentric as a Theory of Social Work Practise*. Open Journal System Volume 8 (1)

Early, G, Moses, W.J, Wilson, L and Lefkowitz, M. (1994) *Symposium; Historical roots of Afrocentrism*, Academic Questions 7(2) pp44-54

Ekob, E. C and Gaikwad, P. (2015) *the Impact of Andragogy on Learning Satisfaction of Graduate Students*. American Journal of Educational Research Vol # (11) pp1378-1386

Escobar, A. (2010) *"Worlds and Knowledge Otherwise: The Latin American Modernity/Coloniality Research Program "In Globalization and the Decolonial Option*. London: Rutledge

Fanon, F. (1967) *"The Negro and the Language". Black Skin, white mask*. Penguin

Garlake, P.S. (1973) Great Zimbabwe; *New Aspects of Archaeology*. London; Stein and Day Publishers

Grosfoguel, R. (2013) *The Structure of Knowledge in Westernized Universities; Epistemic Racism/Sexism and the Four Genocides/Epistemicides of the Long 18th Century*. Human Architecture, Journal of the Sociology of Self Knowledge Vol 11(1)

Grosfoguel, R. Hernandez, R and Velasquez, E. (2016) *Decolonizing Westernized University: Interventions in Philosophy of Education from Within and Without*, University of California.

Hauntondji, P (1997) *Endogenous Knowledge; Research trails*, Dakar: Edition du CODESRIA

Hetela, S. (2016*) Decolonization of Higher Education; Dismantling Epistemic Violence and Eurocentrism in Europe*

Hume, D. (1986) *A treaties of Human Nature*. Oxford. Claredon Press

Hwami, M and Kapoor, D. (ND) *Neo-Colonialism, Higher Education and Student union activism in Zimbabwe*. University of Alberta, Edmonton, Canada.

Ignatieff, M. (2014) *Fire and Ashes. Success and Failure in Politics*. Cambridge. Harvard University Press

Itelela, S. (2016) *Coloniality in our universities and we must urgently decolonize. Mail and Guardian Africa Best Read*, https;//mg.co.za/article/2016, accessed on 18 September 2017.

James, G.G.M. (1954) *"Stolen Legacy". The Egyptian Origins of Western Philosophy*, Texas; Martino Fine Books

Kapuya, Z. (2018; B.Sc. dissertation) *An analysis of the role played by universities in decolonizing higher education in post-colonial Zimbabwe. A case study of Midlands State University 2010-2014.* Midlands State University

Karsenti, T. (2009) *Pedagogical use of ICT Teaching and Reflecting Strategies,* Ottawa; IDRC.
Knowles, M. (1975) *Self-Directed Learning*; Chicago; Follet
_____(1980*) the Adult Learners: A Neglected Species;* Third Edition. Houston. Gulf Publishing.
_____(1984) *Andragogy in Action.* San Francisco; Jossey-Bassey.
Leary, (2009*) A Problem Based Learning Meta-Analysis: Differences across Problem Types, Implementation types, Disciplines and Assessment level.* The interdisciplinary journal of problem-based learning
Mafa, O and Ndudzo, D. (2016) *Andragogy Implications of the Changing Student Enrolment Patterns at the Zimbabwe Open University.* Journal of Business and Management Volume, 18(17) pp&2-77 www.iorsjournals.org.
Mahomva, R.R. (2014) *Pan Africanism, From Cradle, Present and Future,* Leaders of Africa Network
Maldonado-Torres, N. (2016) *Outline Ten Thesis on Coloniality and Decoloniality.*
Mandani, M. (1998) *Citizen and Subject: Contemporary Africa and the Legacy of Late Colonialism;* Kampala; Makerere University
Masisi, K. (2016) *"Stripped of my Dignity and Integrity Hence I can No longer breathe".*
Mazrui, A and Mazrui, A. (1998) *Power of Babel, Language and Governance in Africa,* Chicago: Chicago University Press.
Mazrui, A. (2002) *Africanity Redefined.* Chicago; Chicago University Press

Masaka, D. (2016) *The Impact of Western Colonial Education on Zimbabwe, s traditional and post-colonial educational system* (PhD Thesis, University of South Africa)

Mazama, A. Ed (2003) *The Afrocentric paradigm.* Trenton; Africa World Press.

Mbembe, A.J. (2016) *Decolonizing the University; New Directions, Arts and Humanities in Higher Education,* Volume 15(1) 29-45

McKinney. (2017) *Language in Power in Post-Colonial Schooling; Ideologies in Practise,* New York; Routledge

Mlambo, A.S. (2005) *Post-colonial Higher education in Zimbabwe; The University of Zimbabwe, A Case Study1980-2004.* African Historical Review 37(1) pp107-130

Mignolo, W. (2011) *The Darker Side of western Modernity: Global Futures, Decolonial Options,* Durham; Duke University Press

Mignolo, W. (2011) *Geopolitics of Sensing and Knowing On (De) Coloniality, Boarder Thinking, and Epistemic Disobedience.* Transversal Text Journal.

Mignolo, W.D and Walsh, C.A. (2018) *On Decoloniality; Concepts, Analytics and Praxis.*

Munhande, C and Nciizah, E. (2013) *'Perpetuating Colonial Legacies; Reflections on Post-Colonial African States' development trajectories, Observations from Zimbabwe.* International Journal of Humanities and Social Science Invention. Volume 2 (11) pp10-15. Accessed at www.ijhssi.org.

Mungazi, D. (1993) *Educational policy and National Character; Africa, Japan, The United States and the Soviet,* Ct Prager.

Muparari, T. (ND) *Examine Knowles Conceptualization of Andragogy showing its relevance to the andragogy situation.*www.academia.edu/122226346

Musarurwa, C. (2011) *Teaching with and Learning through ICT's In Zimbabwe's Teachers Education Colleges,* US-China Education Review A

Mpondi, D. (2017) *the politics of National Culture and Urban Education Reforms in Post-Independent Zimbabwe.* International Handbook of Urban Education in Zimbabwe

Mpondi, D. (2004) *Educational Change and Cultural Politics; National Identity-Formation in Zimbabwe.* College of Education of Ohio University

Nair, R. (2013*) Drums Beat All Night,* Cape Town. University of Cape Town Press.

Ndhlovu-Gatsheni, S.J. (2013) *Empire, Global Coloniality and African Subjectivity.* New York; Bingham

Ndhlovu-Gatsheni, S.J. (2013) *Coloniality of Power in Post-Colonial Africa; Myths of decolonization,* Dakar; CODESRIA

Ndhlovu-Gatsheni and Siphamandla, Z. Ed (2016) *Decolonizing the University, Knowledge Systems and Disciplines in Africa,* Kent: Carolina Academic Press.

Nhemachena, A. (2018) *Decolonisation, Afrikanization and Cannibalistic Figure of the Posthuman: Lecture,* College of Humanities; University of Namibia

Oruka, O. H. (1990) *Ethics, a Basic Course for Undergraduate Studies.* Nairobi; Nairobi University Press

Oruka, O. H. (199&) *Sagacious Reasoning,* London; P Lang

Prah, K. (2009) *African Languages, African Development and African Unity.* Lagos; Centre for Black and African Arts and Civilization.

Prah, K. (2016) *Creating Knowledge in Africa; School of Human and Social Science Annual Lectures,* University of Venda 18-20 May 2016

Quinjano, A. (2000*) Coloniality of Power and Eurocentrism in Latin America, International Sociology,* volume 15 (2) pp215-232

Raewyn, C.S. (2016) *Decolonizing Knowledge, Democratising Curriculum,* University of Johannesburg.

Raftopolous, B. (1994) *Zimbabwe; Race and Nationalism in Post-Colonial State.* Harare; SAPES Trust.

Reed, W.E, Lawson, E.J and Gibbs, T. (1997) *Afrocentrism in the 21st Century.* The Western Journal of Black Studies Volume 21 (3) pp73-79)

Riskers, E. (2012) *what is Decolonization and Why Does It Matter. International Cry. A Publication Centre for World Indigenous Studies,* accessed on https//intercontinental cry. Org accessed on 18 September 2017.

Sachikonye, L. (2011) *When a State Turns of Its Citizens. Institutionalized Violence and Political Culture.* Harare; Weaver Press.

Sausa, S. B. (2014) *Epistemologies of the South; Justice against Epistemicide,* London; Routledge.

Sartre, J. P. (1968) *No Exit and Three Other Plays, Dirty Hands, The Files Respectful Prostitute,* New York; Vintage Books

Schele, H. (1997) *an Afrocentric Perspective on Social Welfare,* Philosophy and Policy, Volume 2 (2)

Sertima, I. V. (2003) *Before Columbus. The African Presence in Ancient America,* Washington; Random House Trade paperback

Shizha, E and Makuvaza, N. (2017) *Rethinking Post-Colonial Education in Sub-Saharan Africa in the 21st Century "Post-Millennium Development Goals,* Rotterdam: Boston.

Shizha, E and Kariwo, M.T. (ND) *Education and Development in Zimbabwe. A Social, Political and Economic Analysis;* Rotterdam: Sense Publishers.

Spivak, G. (1994) *Can Subaltern Speak.* Delhi; Stefan Nowotny Publishers

Wa Thiongo, N. (1981) *Decolonizing the Mind, Politics of Language in Africa*. New York; Heinemann

William, C. (1992) *Destruction of Black Civilization*; Chicago; Chicago University Press.

www.ac.msu.ac.zw

Wynter, S. (2015) *On Being and Human Praxis*, London; Duke University Press

Zelig. L. (2008) *Student Politics and Activism in Zimbabwe*. Journal of Asian and African Studies.

Zvobgo, R.J. (1986) *Transforming Education; the Zimbabwe Experience*. Harare; College Press.

Interviews

Dr Richard Muranda (2018), Lecturer at MSU, Department of Music and Musicology

Professor Percslage Chigora (2018), Lecturer at MSU, Department of Politics and Public Management

Dr Godfrey Chikowore (2018), Visiting Lecturer at MSU, Department of Development Studies

Professor Charles Tembo (2018), Lecturer at Midlands State University, Department of African Languages and Culture

D Nkala (2018), Lecturer at MSU, department of Entrepreneurship Studies

Patricia Masiyakurima (2018), Student at MSU, Department of Politics and Public Management

Ngonidzashe Machingauta (2018), An Independent Researcher

Publisher's list

If you have enjoyed *Phenomenology of Decolonizing the University: Essays in the Contemporary Thoughts of Afrikology*, consider these other fine books from Mwanaka Media and Publishing:

Cultural Hybridity and Fixity by Andrew Nyongesa
The Water Cycle by Andrew Nyongesa
Tintinnabulation of Literary Theory by Andrew Nyongesa
I Threw a Star in a Wine Glass by Fethi Sassi
South Africa and United Nations Peacekeeping Offensive Operations by Antonio Garcia
Africanization and Americanization Anthology Volume 1, Searching for Interracial, Interstitial, Intersectional and Interstates Meeting Spaces, Africa Vs North America by Tendai R Mwanaka
A Conversation…, A Contact by Tendai Rinos Mwanaka
A Dark Energy by Tendai Rinos Mwanaka
Africa, UK and Ireland: Writing Politics and Knowledge Production Vol 1 by Tendai R Mwanaka
Best New African Poets 2017 Anthology by Tendai R Mwanaka and Daniel Da Purificacao
Keys in the River: New and Collected Stories by Tendai Rinos Mwanaka
Logbook Written by a Drifter by Tendai Rinos Mwanaka
Mad Bob Republic: Bloodlines, Bile and a Crying Child by Tendai Rinos Mwanaka
How The Twins Grew Up/Makurire Akaita Mapatya by Milutin Djurickovic and Tendai Rinos Mwanaka
Writing Language, Culture and Development, Africa Vs Asia Vol 1 by Tendai R Mwanaka, Wanjohi wa Makokha and Upal Deb

Zimbolicious Poetry Vol 1 by Tendai R Mwanaka and Edward Dzonze
Zimbolicious: An Anthology of Zimbabwean Literature and Arts, Vol 3 by Tendai Mwanaka
Under The Steel Yoke by Jabulani Mzinyathi
A Case of Love and Hate by Chenjerai Mhondera
Epochs of Morning Light by Elena Botts
Fly in a Beehive by Thato Tshukudu
Bounding for Light by Richard Mbuthia
White Man Walking by John Eppel
A Cat and Mouse Affair by Bruno Shora
Sentiments by Jackson Matimba
Best New African Poets 2018 Anthology by Tendai R Mwanaka and Nsah Mala
Drawing Without Licence by Tendai R Mwanaka
Writing Grandmothers/ Escribiendo sobre nuestras raíces: Africa Vs Latin America Vol 2 by Tendai R Mwanaka and Felix Rodriguez
The Scholarship Girl by Abigail George
Words That Matter by Gerry Sikazwe
The Gods Sleep Through It by Wonder Guchu
The Ungendered by Delia Watterson
The Big Noise and Other Noises by Christopher Kudyahakudadirwe
Tiny Human Protection Agency by Megan Landman
Ghetto Symphony by Mandla Mavolwane
Sky for a Foreign Bird by Fethi Sassi
A Portrait of Defiance by Tendai Rinos Mwanaka
When Escape Becomes the only Lover by Tendai R Mwanaka
Where I Belong: moments, mist and song by Smeetha Bhoumik

Nationalism: (Mis)Understanding Donald Trump's Capitalism, Racism, Global Politics, International Trade and Media Wars, Africa Vs North America Vol 2 by Tendai R Mwanaka
Ashes by Ken Weene and Omar O Abdul
Ouafa and Thawra: About a Lover From Tunisia by Arturo Desimone
Thoughts Hunt The Loves/Pfungwa Dzinovhima Vadiwa by Jeton Kelmendi
ويَسهَرُ اللَّيلُ عَلَى شَفَتي...وَالغَمَام by Fethi Sassi
A Letter to the President by Mbizo Chirasha
Righteous Indignation by Jabulani Mzinyathi:
Blooming Cactus By Mikateko Mbambo
Rhythm of Life by Olivia Ngozi Osouha
Travellers Gather Dust and Lust by Gabriel Awuah Mainoo

Soon to be released

Of Bloom Smoke by Abigail George
Denga reshiri yokunze kwenyika by Fethi Sassi
Notes From a Modern Chimurenga: Collected Stories by Tendai Rinos Mwanaka
Tom Boy by Megan Landman
My Spiritual Journey: A Study of the Emerald Tablets by Jonathan Thompson
School of Love and Other Stories by Ricardo Felix Rodriguez
Cycle of Life by Ikegwu Michael Chukwudi
INFLUENCE OF CLIMATE VARIABILITY ON THE PREVALENCE OF DENGUE FEVER IN MANDERA COUNTY, KENYA by NDIWA JOSEPH KIMTAI

Chitungwiza Mushamukuru Wakaenda Kupiko: An Anthology of Chitungwiza Writers and Artists by Tendai Rinos Mwanaka
Best New African Poets 2019 Anthology by Tendai Rinos Mwanaka and Nsah Mala

https://facebook.com/MwanakaMediaAndPublishing/

Printed in the United States
By Bookmasters